REDOUBTED

Makwa Enewed is a sub-imprint of the American Indian Studies Series at Michigan State University Press.

Gordon Henry, *Series Editor*

Makwa Enewed stands dedicated to books that encompass the varied views and perspectives of people working in American Indian communities. In that light, books published under the Makwa Enewed imprint rely less on formal academic critique, argument, methodology, and research conventions and more on experientially grounded views and perspectives on issues, activities, and developments in Indian Country.

While work published in Makwa Enewed may resound with certain personal, speculative, conversational, political, and/or social concerns of individuals and groups of individual American Indian people, in a larger sense such concerns and their delivery reflects the import, strength, uniqueness, and potential viability of the imprint.

The imprint will gather its strength from the voices of tribal leaders, community activists, and socially engaged Native people. Thus, each publication under the Makwa Enewed imprint will call forth from tribally based people and places, reminding readers of the varied beliefs and pressing interests of American Indian tribal people and communities.

REDOUBTED

Poems by
R. Vincent Moniz, Jr.

MAKWA ENEWED • *East Lansing, Michigan*

♾ The paper used in this publication meets the minimum requirements of
ANSI/NISO Z39.48-1992 (R 1997) (Permanence of Paper).

Makwa Enewed
Michigan State University Press
East Lansing, Michigan 48823-5245

Printed and bound in the United States of America.

27 26 25 24 23 22 21 20 19 18   1 2 3 4 5 6 7 8 9 10

Library of Congress Control Number: 2017961948
      ISBN 978-1-938065-07-1 (pbk. : alk. paper)
      ISBN 978-1-938065-08-8 (pdf)
      ISBN 978-1-938065-09-5 (epub)
      ISBN 978-1-938065-10-1 (kindle)

Cover design by Luke Finsaas (www.lfinsaas.com).
Cover photo by OscarPorras/stock.adobe.com.

g green **press** Michigan State University Press is a member of the Green Press
INITIATIVE Initiative and is committed to developing and encouraging ecolog-
ically responsible publishing practices. For more information about the Green
Press Initiative and the use of recycled paper in book publishing, please visit
www.greenpressinitiative.org.

Visit Michigan State University Press at *www.msupress.org*

For you, Always for you.

Contents

Acknowledgments

Without Megan Kate Treinen I would not be a poet, nor anything close to a functioning adult. I would definitely not know love. This book would not be in your hands without her. Busa, every beat of my heart is for you. Nutanuma'kaaki Nuu'etaare waashiraharanito'sh. Nii'aame waateenixkerekak mi'shak owateere omiko'sh. Marcie Rendon and Bao Phi, writers from my neighborhood. I read and listened to your works before I know we were kin. I do not yet belong among the stars with you. The visual artists who let me visit them in their basement apartments and rabbit infested studios. I hold tight every memory, good and bad. Responding to your work gave me strength. Being in your presence gave me hope, truly. To the many women who took pity on me, who still pray and root for me from the treeline. I must pretend your smiles and warmth now but the not paths you carved for us all. To every English teacher, professor, and writing mentor who didn't see a liar, who saw someone who could pull whole worlds out from of the sky above. These few saw what follows this page and knew with guidance, I would grow. Thank you, Teacher of The Flash J. Otis Powell? Mr. Sommers, Mr. Boucher, Mrs. Adamsick, Graham Hartley, Laura Waterman-Wittstock, Sharon Day, Dr. H.e.E., Dr. Buffalohead. Thank you, family, nieces and nephews. I wait for the new ways you will use this to tease me. Hoodfambam, thank you to take in a wet coyote pup when no one else would. Streets of my city, when I had no home, thank you for letting me live on you. I am a different kind of strong for it. Shane Caird, Colin, Stuart Perkins, Jr., Jesse Strong, Noodie, DavidPaul, ElijahDale, Jason T. Dixon, Korto, Katie, lil Lisa S., Giant Killer, Owl, Mikey, Valley Satiavoni Hintzen, Ben Gessner, Rory, Dawn, Melissa, E.B.L., Faye, Gray, Rosemary, Rebecca, Shannon, Sunni, Megan. All friends who made family with me, thank you. To the unseen and the in-between, thank you for showing the shine and the shadow way. To the people of my neighborhood Phillips in Minneapolis, MN, nick-named Cockroach, and divided into East Phillips, thank you to help raise me. If a copy of this collection lands in any of your hands, know that I am just as surprised as you are. They didn't tell us we could do it like this, at all. I'll see you in line at Holy Rosary. We'll chop it up and speak on this then, stay up.

REDOUBTED

12:12:12 12/12/12

During the last long 12
a big dreamer and I
talked about the everyday,
the long road ahead,
and our last best crush.

This explosion particle
hurling through deep
midnight, this rock of life.

We ride it
with the best of them.

This turtle mother holds
us tight, dives down
into an ocean of memory
that sparkles with historic destruction.

She is taking us home, away from
this expanse of twilight and into a cradle
of brilliant lucency.

IT ALL JUST FADES AWAY

World of crazy, imploding Indians,
and the storm of everyone's century.
All of it melts into a boiling pot
of steam and haze. Mr. Wizard
has begun a descent into a volume
bound in Count Chocula
and Franken Berry boxes.

Stories you've never heard
and adventure that no one will believe.
This is a continuing saga and when
called, man, I can't do anything else
but answer.

Come, sit close to an old
friend and warm yourself
by the ember of his memory.
The cold fusion of the season's
change is upon us, and you can't wait
to hear about the time BiG Word
Mom smote an undead faerie
for a literary feast. "It was nuthin'"
she says, "just a preoccupation, my
deer, now eat up."

Edge of your seat as you listen
so hard you don't know your eyes

are closed. Imagine the color of
childhood footie pajamas as I retell
how Coyote wooed 50 buffalo down
Franklin Ave. with nothing but her bike,
a hand drum and a determination
that could eat through 5,000 pieces
of fry bread.

These are cherished tales that greet
me informally as I pull up to this table.
When I sit down in front of this computer
it's all I remember. When the furnace
goes out and I can't help but shiver
to keep the fire within stoked, it's all
I want to tell you. Come and hear it
before I become the same granite history
that sits cross-armed at the bottom
of Powderhorn Pond. Swim down to murky
muddy base where snapping turtle still hides
from the trickster. We look up to greenish
brown blurry future as it all just fades away.

BISON HEART

Instead of your breast
I felt your beat as we kissed
our first kisses in a closet
full of dreams and trivia.

You jerk back as I bobbed
my head to the flow of your
macro cosmos. Seven minutes
of heaven, hurling into seven
years of confusion.

Eyes squint at reflection
in our new bathroom mirror.
Move from rural to urban
was the best carnival ride
I'd ever been on. Moving at all
speeds gone in every direction,
dizzy when my Pops shot me
the only advice I'd ever been
given. "Boy, you gotta be tough."
So there in my family's new lodge,
center of the Little Earth projects
I practiced every swear word I knew.
Building armor for the warrior
I might become.

Scent my Nay-Gah's fancy face
powder. One part lavender, all

parts warmth. It was in those brown
dialysis punctured arms that I learned
this rich powdery smell meant she
would keep me from harm and lift
me up far from the darkness below.

My Nuh-Ay began to howl and beat
upon her chest. The Missouri
and Knife Rivers flow from her
into that flowery powder box.
From her I learned that this smell
also meant you could be dragged
kicking and screaming into the deepest
darkest gully.

Listen to your secret soft words
of affection. Those three sounds,
they two-stepped ladies' choice
from perfect red lips deep into long-
lobed brown ears. It was the very first
time someone outside of my family
ever said this to me. Those same
words sting every inch of my body
as you board a plane. Heading
for school on the east coast,
headed out of my life forever.

Taste one bite from a meal called
"Chicken and Grapes." At least
that's what you told me it was called.
As I fought against my stomach
and tongue's disapproval, a phrase
from my Tatekaá popped
into my head. Dung served from love
tastes like bison heart.

I had seconds, and asked if she would
make it again soon.

I remember
I remember
I'm remembered
I'm an ember.

While Boss Wabooz Sits and Thinks

In response to Jim Denomie's Creative Oven

Brushstrokes to blend and fill
the everyday hustle with the world
between our own and the seceded
bits we escape to create.

Boss Wabooz sees it all and is busy
archiving stones on the bridge
that keeps this world and the world
we our imaginations run free on every
level. This whirlwind dream is alive
and playing in the background are all
my dad's favorite worksite cuts, rock
and roll. All this while the destiny sisters
sit quietly in the corner, crocheting
the longest scarf I've ever seen.

Watch amazed as Old Long Ears reaches
into his giant canvas and pulls out
more and more paint, more blending,
not at fever's pace, but steady and full
with frequent stops to acknowledge
the things I cannot yet see.

Make way to keystone and say out loud
on the bridge to our creative selves
10,000 wishes to every cover of distraction
that keeps us separated from art and work.

We hail every member of the Dire Straits,
all the cuts they played, and anyone who
closed their eyes on 11th and Franklin
and missed a new Indian headed
for the old pow wow just on the other side
of the dream world.

While Old Long Ears paints the connectivity,
close my eyes and tell a story about an echo
of a shadow that used to call me brother.
Today I miss her and hold tears back
when remembering one morning I shaved
all my man hair off and she called to me

"There's my little brother, oh I missed you,
sweet boy, sit here and tell me the story
of us, never forget we are forever. Juniorbugg,
don't let your mind toss me to the back
with complicated math and rules of white
people's words. Keep me as I am today,
keep me close to the memory of car keys
and what your true name is."

While Boss Wabooz sits and thinks
about the glue of our worlds, write
this and remember every face she has ever
made, and when I look up with snot and tears,
see the story of all of us, clear as yellow
sunflowers leaning in all directions
trying to find the warmth of the Sun
in cold gray skies.

On the Cusp of Change, Dream Just Hard

Run, not for health, in the scared way
while mix and make haste feeds my
want to escape, my family and I get on
a train that looks like a tram,
we don't speak,
just look back at the rugged station
wagon that we called home.

We are not relieved.

The bottom of the train is glass and we
are 10 stories up from the world
and can see all the page ends.
Pass over prairie and butte, gully
and riverbed.

My mother inhales sharply and points
down past the floor windows to her
mother and the dirt floor of the log cabin
she came from. Passed by fast enough
to wonder what's next but not slow enough
to want to jump off.

Cold rushes to meet our skin, and in a flash,
moments and landscapes from our shared
timeline pass underneath us well within our
eyesight but just out of reach.

Look up and wonder where we are all going
and why we are all so filled with worry and doubt.
Look down at my feet and past them, past the glass
past the bird's eye of these memories.

The train halts midair over my family's
second Southside home midwinter
just after the sun had set.
See my dad's work van driving up
and realize why the train is still,
equal to our own controlled quiet.

The van doesn't stop, not in this memory
or the variations I will make up that night.
Just in front of the house, this old van
births a pine tree out onto the street and
doesn't stop moving.

The van keeps going, in this history,
tell myself that the van and my dad
are both in separate arguments with my ma
and neither wanted to be berated this night,
so they tucked tail, discharged a family
puzzle piece and fled.

The train starts to move just as younger
me comes out from the darkness to grab
the newest offering of guilt up from the street.
That night I remember not wanting to look
at my dad's taillights again, so I looked up
where all my dreams lived and gave thanks
to anyone dumb enough to take pity on me.

He never stopped, never asked why because
I knew the reason.

Mumma shakes me, says I'm cold, and tries
to warm my shoulders as this train slows,
comes to the end of the line where a giant
castle of a house on a huge mountain
overlooks a countryside I've only seen
in movies.

Stumble off in unison and move into the darkness
of this new scene. This drum and dance
troupe of us have come in the back entrance
of I don't know where and are staring
at couches and dimly lit hallways.

Park on a sofa that looks like my Uncle
Hooligan's and just before this one ends,
see everyone who isn't there get up
and move away from us.
Backs to fronts,
slowly move into the darker rooms
and hallways in front of us
lighting the way with shared dreams
and kinship responsibility.

Wake up and hear bird chirps, cars,
my own voice echoing away from me

"Miss you, miss you, miss you . . ."

In The Last Village's Gym

Courts in my neighborhood
are impossibly small. Just enough
room for eight Indin kids to bounce
pass no-lookers, drop a long dime
from the opposition's three-point line,
and charge the cup with smiles
bigger than backboards made
of metal, hope, and plywood.
Just wanted to remember today
is all.

Paper-bag colored girls and boys
who decided that the game
did not need the score to be kept
to play with all they've got.
Kids who foul harder than pros
they emulate, offer condolences
by rubbing and patting wounds
they just created.
These young gods of war
and tenderness know all the best
ways to lay down eagle staff
and shield. In the smallest gym
in the heart of The Last Village
I get after myself for coveting
the magics of a tribe I left
when I turned 11. Saw my father's
piss-soaked pants after too many
days bent trying to hide his hurt.

Heard rage spit and roar out
of mother volcano who
would enable Old Scratch
himself if it meant she would
never be left alone.
Eleven, the age I sewed
the matchstick mask
to my fat, unremarkable
face. Eleven, when I lost youth-
filled medicine bag these eight
brown basketball Americans
flaunt and fly that which I traded
for the adult I thought
I was supposed to become.

THE FIRST RULE

Get back and feel the imposed
calm. Like back in the way back
when I was still giant-eyed
and full of potential.

Gray blurry memory of some
dummy who didn't understand
the first rule. That prey becomes
food, and that food becomes waste,
but not in the lila wia wastè way.

In an ugly alley on the Southside
of things, my friend Chicky
and I see how the big boys run.
Clothes clinging to sweat, clinging
to skin.

The old howl of new defeat.
We watch them stop mid-display,
brush themselves off, and fade
into the darkness as if the lesson never
needed to be taught.

I see their potential flicker out
like lightning bugs as it falls harder
than the unlearned just did.
Motionless I watch their timelines

of good fortune fade to an empty
and now whisper-quiet street, only
sound is coming from The Commodore's
old beat-up jukebox.

My friend looks up at me and then squints
hard into the night. Chicky sees a new
way out of the darkness and begins
walking into the alley.

Never looks back at me to say his goodbyes.

SECEDED URBAN LANDS

Sit in my whip like last lonely hustler
waiting outside of packed event.
Just too Indi-on-ish to get within
speaking distance of so many.

Posted up where the people
trade handshakes and laughs
for tough looks and yells.
Here I write where fast glances
help protect against

an inevitably. This is where
the youngest and oldest
fight for one quarter and the right
to help move food from store to trunk.

I scribble as quick as I can, catch
as many stories I can hear.

Change is coming to take the old
history books with them.
Ancient stories share with new
toys, still mint in box.

An ambassador making presidential
moves. The urgency to archive
has filled me recently, and now
I don't know if I can stop.

The Ave. is alive. On this day,
we are the balance we strive
for. We are the road only we walk,
red and brown
from our blood and feces.

Today it feels great and horrible
to be capital "I" Indin. After
another 24-hour wake to send
home another Indigenous youth.
Sing a song for a boy who danced
on too early. Will wake before the sun,
look up and count him among his relatives
in the Star World.

Mourning death while celebrating rebirth,
we find a new way to shuffle up and down
our seceded urban lands. Count each other
among current survivors of systematic genocide
blended into the corners of community.

BENSON FORMATION

My uncle, youngest son to a family
of memory champions.

I know him, but I don't know him.

At celebrations of our continued survival,
my Uncle, govern of the moon,
is there directing familiar symphony.

Kaw-Liga holds our traditions on his
back. A liver-colored Atlas, well versed
in heavy kinship responsibility,
replacing his knees many times
from the pressure,

he holds strong.

This Benson formation,
umber as oak leaves, Uncle
was made as a reflection of the land
of our people,
lower shale, middle dolomite,
upper shale, and hard as forged steel.

We hold on.

Uncle, older brother of my mumma
with solid connections to our history.
I don't know him well, but that sadness
changes every time I work up the courage
to visit. Every time I'm there hear a new
story about brothers and sisters
who danced Home too early.

Our Kaw-Liga is self-made but doesn't hide
"S" under Pendleton vest. Doesn't need a phone
booth to quick change my perception of him.
He carries my heart on the songs he sings to me.
Words of my grandmother, tongue of One of Us,
sewn together by the gentle strumming of his guitar.

This is not the man I grew up with living
less than two miles away from.

This man of harsh winter and boiling
summer was a mystery held in front
of me by snuff-colored governess.

As time dances us two-handed
around the circle,
we break down seasons
of unpronounced connection.

Not here to tell you
whoppers and myths about him,

Here to remind you that we thrive,
and that this man,
is a blueprint for our continued
Permanence.

WHO IS COYOTE?

I've known Coyote forever.
My sisters were friends with him back in the day, could hear
them cracking jokes out in the yard all summer. He told them
that he would show them the hustle, the grand scheme of
things. He made them promise not to fall in love with him. He
told them that he had already promised himself to the moon,
and had been chasing her all night.

They laughed.

Coyote used to pull up to Bob Thunder while he was on duty and
try to race in a stolen whip down Bloomington. He'd wait
for the right moment, just before the light would turn green.
Then he'd pull up, rev the engine and laugh so loud the whole
projects could hear him, and bam just like that, he'd take off!
Never seen Thumper arrest him, but I did hear him yell: "Go Home!" or
"Quit Messing Around!"

He laughed.

Last time I saw Coyote, he was in rough shape, still called me shorty.
He told me my sisters were sacred, that it's all special—every
last bit of it, and that even the buffalos on The Ave. need you to
look them in the eye; they deserve it; we all do. He told me he
tricked Wah Wah Teh Go Nay Ga Bo into giving him that big piece
on the Indin center. Showed me a picture of him and Mr. Morrison
both shaking hands; Mr. Morrison looked pissed.

We laughed.

He told me he had some shit to take care of, but he'd be around.
He said to come by sometime and meet his Wia. He loved
her because she was beautiful, knew all his tricks, and smelled
like sweet grass and ozone. He made me promise not to fall in love
with her, that he'd been chasing her his whole life.
Last thing I heard him say was

"I'll see you in line at Holy Rosary, stay up." I laughed.

2477-365

A community of children, sacred gift
from great mystery, we fail you.
Sewn together, we are a neighborhood
of neglected patchwork that warms no one.
New news trickling in, more gray sons
become food for the machine. Ground out
into prison cell shaped patties, these
Naturals of The Club where mob is distorted
into radioactive comfort food.

These are Icarus children who burn too
bright as they fell through cracks
in social services
while falling through the cracks
in their families.

A community now swims away from
their creation. Ashamed of our shared
truth, crabs in a barrel can never see
sons, nephews, dads, or uncles
when they search for the star path
home under clouded sky.

These men and I
run parallel in a neighborhood
that spits out statistics and myth.
Sons of the trickster, we are lost

and rage-filled lessons
that no one seems to be learning from.
We now follow in line
into a darkness named double-edged sword.

Wished for a Year of It

Winter has
decided to mirror
my heart. Beat of deep tragedy,
pump in spite of the shallow bits
of oxygen fed to it.

Winter has
decided that it's like my knees,
cinnamon rolls shuckin' to old-
time rock and roll, painted up
and ready for the next dance.

Winter has
no place else it
would like to go to, all of its relatives
live 6–8 hours away, only enough
gas money to make it
part the way.

Winter has
given up, will no longer
control itself while you are out
to dinner and a movie. It has decided
to sing and dance wherever
it pleases, doesn't care if you know
the steps or the song anymore,
it just wants to feel crooked release

from the bottom of its naked feet
and open toothless mouth.

Winter has
had its fill of travel,
wants to be from where you are
from again, doesn't care what you
think about it, only wants your two-finger
salute as you pass each other
on the frontage road
of a radioactive tomorrow.

THE WIND OF THIS WAY

Curves?
No these aren't curves, these are the backroads that wind through my
    reservation.
Roads that dance into a pair of jeans made of the plains, these arteries
are dangerous and deadly.

From sweet delicate ankle twist to mischievous sharp
turn of a grin, these trails are seldom driven at night. As the sun
sets, its path becomes uncontainable. Sway to a whispered
rhythm. A silent writhe and contort, these routes change
in a night that is darker than 40 boiled owls.

These roads that are not roads will only be traveled
on by the adventurous, the brave, and the illest
of women and men.

The roadside is monument to the unworthy:
flowers and tokens of remembrance
to those who did not respect this passage.

These curves that are not curves follow
the movement of the snake people.
Coming out of their homes
to find a better place
in the warmth and glow
of the sun.

Heard Your Buffalo on The Ave.

Two-dreams whispers one
into my giant-lobed ears.
A short, skinny one with pitiful
magic that can only blend
and shade themselves into
the foreground of a mural
I've yet to paint on the ceiling
of the All Nations Indian Church.

Wake up in my grandmother's
long gone log cabin. Swear I hear
that sweet, wonderful woman
walking around sprinkling water
on her dirt floor to keep it all
in line.
Think about summer, cool old
Indin men who told me stories
about the sadness of war
and victory of defeat. This Dan George
look-alike chuckles and rubs his
boney hands together as I beg
for just one more story about a man
named Goes Behind with ponies
built from mercury and smoke.

It's cold now, my fingers and nose
feel like beeswax spread and left
out in sub-zero January air

to freeze and become brittle
from dreams of dreams.
Faint echo coming from the back
of a cave drips onto a winter count
that will be lost in a tragic accident.
This unrecoverable memory map
will burn bright blues, greens,
and with white hot heat it will sear
until it blends and shades itself
into the foreground of Franklin Avenue.

Just like all the other sacred brown buffalo.

Chubby Shoulders

*Look real deep in my eyes and jump on my back because I'm
gonna take you through the wall! And when you look at these
veins the only thing that flows through these veins is the
power of the warrior! Aaaaaaaaa!*
—The Ultimate Warrior

The world, held on sun-kissed curved
shoulder, was once a tiny rural town,
camp grounds, and three city neighborhoods
wide. Memory of tiny me is kept alive
by single diminishing coal who shook
and grunted like any madman colored
in an angry neon spectrum would.

Elementary balance of a full-time urban
Indian kid. Was learning to move
like the grass to the beat of my heart
while getting into my first 100 fistfights
in defense my long, curly, black hair. My
climb up included a warrior who raged
out to me from too old TV screen
like bat light over dark city skyline.

Alone, where I would not have to explain
to either world where only moonwalking
would do, I wished for grassdance
regalia that mimicked his color and flare.
My brain exploded at the idea of being
painted up. The regular geometry
of my tribe would not do. Could see
no better design than his upside down
"W" bursting at its seams with wild
slashes of color.

This was an emblem so powerful,
members from the Wu-Tang Clan
would later emulate on skin
and albums.

This son with mother who wore pink
mohawk in her grocery getter almost
danced onto the pow wow scene
like a warrior from an alien world,
but that is a "why not" for a different day.

Hurt Back

With over-the-counter pain meds my bed became landing pad of the craziest dream ever.

Hiding from a Credible Hulk with my turtle-colored glasses on in my uncle's basement. My cousin pulls up in his white stallion of a pickup while another Twin Buttes face covers us from the truck bed with the biggest crossbow I'd ever seen. It got much weirder, but when I was listening to my own recounting I decided that no ever needed to hear those stories.

When Frank Yellow Jumped Out of History to Hand Me an American Spirit

Two regular old, gray-socked, fry bread–smelling, acne-laced Indian boys decided to leap from the orange and black of high school confinement. In the hurly burly of Manish Boyhood, they held in backpacks stories mixed with German industrial machine rise up and truth in classic Bedford-Stuyvesant retelling.

These two branches of kindling from the Indigenous renegade tree took to the wide openness of future and laid by the river to get as much of it written down with pencils they borrowed from their own ancestors.

CREATED BY TRIUMPH AND TRAGEDY

Wall of distrust, each brick
placed by survivors.
Champions who lived,
so we can breathe.

Excuse the raw in me;
it was created by triumph
and tragedy.

WORD MEDICINE

Watched a master share word medicine
happily and evenly with everyone.
Share as if we belong to kinship.
She is a gatherer
fishing for us,
hunting for creation,
placing invisible traps within the cool prairie grass.
Captures our attention in story.
Our shape is small, almost a line, and when she overlaps her
well-crafted circle on our own,

we are enveloped in myth.
In this diagram we crisscross
against lines of Joy,
Strife,
Medicine.

WHEN FIRE REPLACED THEIR EYES

For Jude and Shoni Schimmel

Maybe we all pulled them
out of our collective want
to hit a reverse no-look
layup or toss up a rainbow
from beyond the reservation
line of three, just before the white
border towns of blocked
shots and missed opportunity.

Every part of our seceded
lands will put up a statue
at these crossroads of
"them" and "us" to remember
when Chess and Checkers
Schimmel picked up
the game of legend
and immorality,
and rested 3.3 million hopes
and dreams on their
square brown backs.

This c&c run and gun
factory will open up
Dreams and possibilities
for the next 500 years.

Their story is already
being crafted in new

and old oral tradition.
Look out into the network
of us and you will see two
sparks of our desire.

When Indins and Indians
talk about the sisters
of hardwood and confederation,
they will speak of the fire
that replaced their eyes.
Much four-day-long stories
will retell about regalia
of red solar flare that
The Sun sewn special
for them.

These two figments
of Indigenous Borg
are growing by feet
and inches. Already counting
coup on the idea of Dr. Naismith's
version of an Indigenous game
that has been played here
for millennia, they round dance
the history of our game back
into a lexicon of The Game.

Chess and Checkers
Schimmel don't have to win
any more games; legends
like them, just have to make
one, eyes closed, toss up
of a shot in front of the world and sink it. All they have to do is get
knocked down and rise up with searing heat and passion.
These warriors of kicked-in door

only need one shot, one release
of spinning orange sacred to pierce millions
of beating red and brown hearts.

Upper Seward

The older women who make up the majority
in this neighborhood can smell big change
coming up from the Mississippi. Women
who kept this L-shaped community together
have packed up and moved on for even greener
pastures than this. Sisters of a Habit, railing
against war on the same bridge every weekend.
You've seen them, maybe even honked a horn in support
of people standing over a river on a street named Lake.

The first spring after their escape, I see four tulips
pop up in four different places in their magical yard.
Laughing at the comfort of it,
four tulips, four wonderful sisters.
Head down into my basement and pop in a vhs
tape of these good people talking about sisterhood,
their faith
and the love they share for mankind.

Change of wind is aching former glory
and when news comes that the nicest
neighbor ever has to move out of the apartment
above us, a new note forms in the song
of this hidden ore of a neighborhood. This woman,
who was once the head of a university's
day care center, a woman who literally
looked after and cared for our future,
now has to move out her home of 26 years

because her assistance said she has one too
many rooms in a tiny-roomed apartment.
This kind, always smiling woman walked
on the very first AIM patrol and saw the very
first Indigenous contemporary dancers
in Phillips, dancing to singers and drum
on a recorded tape, because none of the Natives
here knew the songs were living inside their hearts.

This woman's life is a part of our rise up,
and as she rushes around above me
trying to pack her and her daughter's history
into cardboard, everything slows, and I wonder
if the days will be as bright when it will be our turn
to get pushed out of diamond-encrusted tragedy.

Hope the new neighbors know they are living in lodges
of good history and happy magic.

FLIGHT IN A PAWN SHOP

BiG Stu found some fly wings in a pawnshop
on the exact day the owners decided to give 1/3
of their hoard away. They walked up to the man
mountain and asked him if he could walk away
clean with any one thing in the store, what would
it be?

BiG told them he loved the shine of the 100 spokes
by the front door. With those four slabs of chrome
and rubber he'd slide all over the south side
of things. If he had a car he'd leave with a sound
system that could set off car alarms at least
six blocks away. Told them all the movies he'd choose
that starred unknowns with stories that stayed
with him like all his best memories.

Impressed, the owners decided to give Treebeard
everything he had just asked for. Stuart W. Perkins Jr.
had just opened the door to desire, looked inside eyes
wide open, and seen the Sun shine on him. This brown
juggernaut closed this door, waved his hand, told them
to strap those wings tucked under glass to his back
and he'd be on his way.

You can see him when the moon has eaten its fill.
He's out there, flying and wishing for it all.

SKINS! IN! SPACE!

Indians of the final frontier,
lineal descendants of silver-
screened stereotype. Hear
the nonprofit bookstore flute
music as they enter, stutter step
from shuttle bay 2. In a house where
every turn of the knob was hotly
contested, their stories were coveted
dream and adventure.

How could I be expected to look
away? These were chronicles
that matched an epic oral tradition.
Grand substitutes for storytelling
that could only be told in winter
circles of wonder. Snowless,
this elementary school maniac watched
TNG reruns year round.

And then came *Voyager* and the beginning
of a distinction carved between
a world that was new and fantastic,
but also full of old intergalactic
Indian stereotype. Funneled into one
character, Chakotay is filled to the
brim with every adage from the lie
and legend of the TV Indian.

The culture of this walking
sensitivity training is a patchwork
of token Indian mysticism. A face
tattoo that ties him to a vague myth
of magical made-up Indians.

The ink
is actually a signal to everyone that
this man is now an adult Indigenous
woman from the West Coast.
No New Age ritual here, his religion
is a mix of Northern Plains, and his
spirit guide can be reached on a gift
from the 24th-century Native American
Church, because sacred is always
just a touch of technology away.

This mashup of tired untruths
has been recast from renegade
savage to wizardly sage because
even racism is supposed to have depth.
Tribal enrollment that changes like
clean socks, every Indian is the same
Indian is a scream that can be heard,
even in space.

Star Trek, you and the
10th grade me are still in a fight
because of "The Generi-kee."

Spins a First Snow Story

Donna Moe at the table reading
bones. Enjoying the what ifs,
laughing eyes closed in between
the in-between. An everyday circle
ending another week by the muddy
river.

Elijah Dale spins a first snow story
where everyone gets 15 and 20s, 25s
the legend of 30 stays just someone
else's win. Spotify is on the 1s and 2s
in the background, pushing product
and classics.

These songs with faces take us to other
retellings and unsolved mystery. Back
when we used to be indestructible
superheroes, Power Rangers, and corner
store trickers holding the truth in pockets
full of the evening's next adventure.

If I Was a Chairman

Fly every legendary Indigenous artist
here to perform. Put the list online
and have the people vote
on who's coming
and when.

Coordinate
with the other chairs,
Indian student orgs, hot-
shot E.D.'s, activists, pacifists, AIMsters.

We'd come together like we do when blue
moons break out over this urban electric
Rez. St. Paul lodging and Minneapolis
meals would be all set up far
and way in advance.

Would take over all
my other meetings talking
about the next performance. We'd wait
at the airport with signs, wave at the Indians
whose stories make us stronger. We'd round
dance on the tarmac and make everyone
else 30 minutes late to some
other adventure.

Sidewalk Indian Holiday Greeting

Now to the task at hand, Operation Shake That Smoke has begun. WE RIDE! Happy Holidays to each and every one of you. To everyone who can't make it Home this year, hunkering down in apartments, lofts, tents, and sometimes houses, center in on whatever you call your small land in trust, places where Home hangs like memory folded-in story and DANCE YOUR STYLE!!!!!!

A History Nicknamed Cockroach

My hood that's no longer a hood.

This place is a pristine, polished,
gentrified condo farm. My memories
are there, squeezed between clean
new buildings, filled with people
who will never ever buzz me into them.

Even The Roach has a jazzy new makeover,
and The Peacemaker Center?
Just becomes somewhere in my mind.
Our old places
overlap someone's new places,
and around the Venn diagram we all dance,
ladies' choice.

Spend these hurt days gathering the medicine
of my own history on invisible leather. On days
I feel small, it is the giant memories of what once was
that consumes indomitable ingots of frustration.
Curl into the path carved in the streets with my history.

Strong is my medicine and
here I know safety.
Here I know much, and
it is simple.
Here lives a refrain

dancing me backward to songs
only sung by the ghosts
who too called this

Home and home.

Braided and Unbranded

Can hear it all from this cove,
slap of tire to slick tar, laugh,
yell, fight, and piss into mirrors
of our own reflection. Family
of rain has come. They keep
painting.

Rainwater ancestors share
their songs, use the watchful
eye of the Morrison as their

drum, Crow Hop to fancy shawl,
every change up a new opportunity
to dance. And they do.

In motions that hurt my descendants'
knees and ankles,

I write and they paint.

Whirlpool of our mini cosmos
and we are in its eye. Not quiet,
not quite safe, but it's here
and so are we. Old scars, bits
of shoe scuff wiped off with water
that washes away the old count
one beat at a time.

Every kind of siren screams
and rips through The Ave.
These alarms bounce off
of 11 railroad ties used
as steps away and up back
into a pulse of us. This
is a loop in time where every
one I've ever met walks by,
old, young, dead, or alive. They wave
and give me the good trade salute.

They keep painting. The story,
only partly written down is coming
outta their aerosol-filled fingertips.
Members of the community stop
and tease, fill this tiny space
with together. And then? Gone.

COSMIC EVENTIDE OF GRACEFUL MOVEMENT

Maria Tallchief (January 24, 1925–April 11, 2013)
was the first Native American to become prima ballerina.
Condolences to the Tallchief family. She will be greatly
missed but never forgotten. A true role model for all artists.

This winter has extended itself
this year. One-dog night sings
their traveling song loud
with air and water.

This year they do not sing only
for their movement to other region.

This song stretches, reaches,
and blasts chilled spine,
creates a land bridge from here
out to unknown mass
of twinkle and cosmic eventide
of graceful movement.

Beauty of ice and snow
has come to take one of their clan
home and have offered the gift
of white buffalo calf robe,
an unmarked Pendleton for the
journey Home.

This blanket, covers and radiates,
soothes with blinding brilliance.

It is time for our ancestors to enjoy
this cherished one and dance for the people
among the stars.

SING LOUD

Sang vocables after everyone
left. Heard the house move in unison,
creaking, keeping the beat.
Sang after no one, without
meaning. All the phrases
in my memory
are for other things.

So my songs today
are for my own worn memory.
Tired but wrapped in the thoughts
of good people who
sang about old world
victory surrounded
by new world defeat.

Sing loud, without embarrassment, because my mind
is strong today. In a harmony
that few can appreciate,
a good memory song
has permeated this
neighborhood.

Clear my throat,
and the song is already
invisible. I never imagine
who will sing next or what,
if anything at all, will be sung. No,
my thought is only "who will sing to remember me?"

HEADED OUT

I'm walking again, always away from something
> An argument
> Trouble
> A really bad smell.

It's cold and my feet are not my feet; they belong to my grandmother
> now, my Nay-Gah Blanche Benson.

The wind hits me so hard I forget where I'm going and I put my
> thumb on the roof of my mouth.

With my other hand I pull out my harmonica, but only think about
> playing.

I look at it to remind me
> of good times
> of warm afternoons at the falls
> of you and me smiling as we stare into the sun, becoming
>> blind to the warmth of our own hearts.

Gently singing a 49 as we melt in the sunset's rays.
> When the sun goes down
> won't you dance with me;
> we'll go round dancing all night.

The warmth of that memory propels me past this cold season and into
> better days.

All Systems Nominal

It's downward spiral season, because
the balance, she loves a good year
long story about rising from ashes
we help ignite. An acknowledgment
of change, or the sharp turn from sullen
stretch of long staying winter to places
green with new life with more joy
than a Crock-Pot full of blue jays
and cardinals.

HOUSE AND A HORSE

Pack eight suitcases in an apartment
that is almost a decade behind me.

Everything color coordinated
and I'm rushing around
for no reason. Then, the building
tilts and everything dances out
grand entry–style, flags and all,
out like a poured box of cereal.

Fall onto a back parking lot
and run because now the sweat
on my forehead says I'm late
for the train. At least, it feels
that way.

When the weird reasons to zip
have slowed, wake up, walk out
into the living room. Stare at the orange
line on the horizon until my eyes water,
at this line of duality, let myself
wonder at the spider strings
connecting us all.

There in my living room, an inch off
the hardwood, wonder aloud
at the altar of will. Will I ever dream of her

face again and the stars she keeps in her skin?
Will I burn my wings and lament
cloudless day as it teases me
about buying plane tickets to places
I don't care to see? Will I ever wake up,
or must I dance forever here forever?
Will I ever slow and tire,
if I ever let go of invisible reins,
throw back my arms and head
like Lieutenant John Dunbar
in the movie *Dances with Wolves*?

Let them give me a horse and a house
far away from busy work dreams so that nothing
will break my concentration. Let it be far
enough away so that only Graham Greene
and Rodney Grant will want to bother me
and trade me stories for a saddled and broken-
down me.

High Plains Drifter Pugilism

If I were not afraid, I'd grassdance
to the center of my neighborhood.
On the way, I'd say hi to all my
neighbors, chuck deuces
at the gangsters, and *Top Gun*
high-five every last one of the hustlers.
On down the avenue I'd spin
and spin, a flailing mix of smiles
and chaos.

If I were not afraid, I'd stop, and go
to the Home of my heart. When I got
there, I'd say goodbye to all the lost
smiles and chaos buried in old wood
boxes above and below Bird Woman's
lake. I'd hug sisters and brothers
that are hours and infinities away.

If I were not afraid I'd listen to stories
that take days to tell. I'd get teased
everywhere and way possible until
I take off this poetry flint knife
I've been sharpening and pick up
a wit that the Nu-Eta have been slinging
as if High Plains Drifter pugilism
was religion.

If I were not afraid, when I got
to the center of my neighborhood,
when I could swim as close to ancestors
who were a part of our 3rd displacement,
I'd look up to the sky world and thank
all that is for this day and every day
before, then,

I'd fly.

SEEKERS

Tucked emotions in my dad's old
canvas backpack and set out to see
the world.

With 180 dollars rolled tight
on the inside pocket of my uncle's
jacket, I took off with my ma's best
hairbrush and 1,000 rubber bands.

On a day that would be remembered
as regular, I looked squinty eyed
at the biggest truck I had ever seen.

Maude was the rig's owner and pushed
that wreck like she was trying to break
a world speed record. She stood three foot
two inches, but inside the cab she looked
like the general of a giant army.

When we had gone down the last road
we could, I hopped out and told her
I'd see her down the line. Maude looked
down at me and then back to the road
ahead and said,

"Seein' is for visionaries son, you and I
are seekers of life's great mystery, don't

let me catch you seein' when you could
be seekin'."

Watched those lights turn to embers,
flicker and fall. Looked forward full
of story and thirst for the next adventure.

When I Danced a Manifold Destiny from Boss Wabooz

Muted morning of naked bliss

share cha-cha-cha with finely braided break of night
at the ramp of light gray
in bold between the season change
when blue purple morphs to red and orange.

In this basecoat is when I heard the light tap tap tap
at my back apartment door.
Dress and peek through hole where glances are snuck at the door-

to-door hustlers.
Today the thumping continued, but as my eye filled the shallow fisheye
could not catch a glimpse of what was on the other side of the door.

For a moment, thought that it might be in my head, that from here on out
my heart would demand the attention it deserved. This was quickly
        laughed
away when after the tapping stopped and my name echoed off of the
        hallway behind me.

Open the door to find rabbit with wings. Fluttering and busy as a
        humming bird. It had made itself comfortable and cleaned my
        entire back porch.
I caught this bunny off guard, and when door became burst of action it
        flew around my head.

It had with it a note, and quickly this now silent mythic animal floated
in front of me with a smile bigger than any one of my nieces and
nephews.

The note was hand written, it simply said

"follow him."

Like that, the bird-bunny spun out and hit the end of the alleyway.

I fell over from trying to get my shoes on quick.

In the car, I watched this bunny zig, zag, and do cartwheels while
laughing and
zinging in and out of traffic.
We hit the highway and

road down road we traveled
into smaller highway,
into smaller byway,
into frontage road,
into dirt.
Then I saw a sign telling me to steer clear of ordinary.

The car wouldn't go any farther,
we had reached a small line
made of packed down dirt.
Out of the whip, into a path
that was smaller than I would
ever be. Could hear music
down the gulley and up high
onto a butte that shouldn't be there.

The two-step beat hit me, and on instinct
started to round dance with the new world
around me. Forward into smaller and smaller
versions of the bunny and myself until we
reached this new world.

The bunny and I were the same size now
and because everything thing matched our size
I took tea on the porch and watched
amazed as my old rocking horse lined
up with rocking horses from all dreams
of missing that one perfect pony.

Heard a gun ring out, and they were off.
Angel bunny walked back over to me,
now big as I, however it seemed
to be without its speed.

Handed me a soda and said the first
words beyond my own faint name
in a kitchen I don't think was mine
anymore.
"Boss is upstairs waiting."
It sat down, pretended I wasn't
there anymore and told my rocking
horse to

"RUUUUUUUUN!"

The climb I was making to meet Boss Wabooz
danced in and out of reality. It seemed
like the staircase was never-ending.
On a slider that didn't seem to slide, I was walking
against the escalator. Just as I thought about going back
to see if my rocking horse had won, I made it to the top

of the whirl. Looked out window to see the everything
of down below.

I had traveled to where the here and now
blended with the magics in the corner
of my mind. Watched excited from this window
as slugbugs with horns grazed
in open field like buffalo.

In the tornado of awe realized
I had come to the Magic Maker
and had not even brought an offering.
Decided to offer up a wink
from the butte hiding the first light
when I left my home by the river, electric.

Old Long Ears accepted my gift
happily but before one whisper
could escape, He raised one finger,
leaned back into his bison hide
Barcalounger, and pointed
to the champions race back below.

This was my first time traveling
to Boss Wabooz and his plot of magics
just beyond the edge of my own pitiful reality.

MY STEREOTYPE CAME TO ME IN A DREAM

Wooden hollow flute and rain sounds
CD opened my eyes.
My stereotype is in the kitchen
making mac and cheese.
Telling me to be stoic.

Check bones cut from granite,
eight-pack stomach, and caped-crusader
chest. His muscles had muscles.

Neon green feathered headdress
so big it wrapped around his body
like a snake. Advised me to be quiet
and strong but that my butt
needed work.

WE DANCE IN OUR SLEEP

My left hand remembers when it led
the way. Wears darkness like a glove,
reboots muscle memory, and begins
to make what-if jumpers from 15 feet
away. Wake as the last convulsion
subsides, extend to grab at the outline
of perfect form.

Her legs want to run and dance.
Under two star blankets her thin pale
limbs kick out to a beat made by filled
lungs. Slow and direct, in and out.
Legs seize with exhaustion, she is still
as postcard lakes. Glance at the line
her body makes in the darkness, reach
out to hold shape.

Duluth/Superior

Duality in a Honda Accord, racing around
ground zero of Zed's revenge. Grease
from double-cooked, triple bacon,
and jalapeño cream cheese burgers
propel us into a night full of dark
and terror.

We know nothing of Jon's snow
solo show deep in the gully of spring.
As the night drifts into a sea of midnight
blues, we become New Age wizards, neo
mystics reading the cracks in these barren
and empty sidewalks, search for futures
that include the best possible evening,
then we ride.

Leave yesteryear's gasolina with the back
monkeys in our hotel rooms. Wave goodbye
to stunning Indians with half-arm tattoos
that echo untold glory. We are two fiends
of story, ready to go look for swords in stones
and round tables to hold a horde of men
only half grown up.

What we find are chillbillies and the streets
they have lived on for as long as they can remember.
New toothless grin inside mouth

of oaken oracle happily tells us of a northern
training ground for woodland ninja.

With eyes bulging, climb to the highest building
on the highest ridge in these towns,
and there under cover of open black cloak
are two bo staffs colored purple and orange.
Pick up these Now and Later–colored weapons
and begin leaping from roof to roof.
This is adventure we just knew we'd find nestled
in caring arms, and we leap with
joy from rooftop to rooftop.

Hear nothing but wind and cheers from the people
below. We are bad neeg ninjas and even worse
at these shadow moves. At last jump of circled
around structure. We stop and quench our thirst
in a lake of broken promises. Our clothes tattered
from the night's neon explosion are taken pity
on by a tailor who just opened up for the day.

She tells me she worked with my uncle Tony
at the casino and asks me to send my condolences
to my father, now the last
of his tribe. Write down her kind words
and as sadness wells up, we begin looking
for an exit. This woman, seeing our plan runs
to the back of her back and pulls out an all-white
tuxedo and tells me my Uncle ToneZone dropped
this off and never returned.

Before I have a chance to protest, I'm already
wearing this albino jacket with tails and the top
hat. Tuck the monocle in my breast pocket, give
the unicorn pants and dress shoes a quick once

over. In gratitude of these fine duds, I sing
"Puttin' on the Ritz" as I dance outta that story
and into the break of dawn and tomorrow.

Tired of stepping out, float
back into nestled body of comfort
and stillness. Wake just as Sun waves
to me from a line just off the horizon.

SUMMER SOLSTICE AND ABORIGINAL DAY

On the longest day ever I celebrated
being brown. Not just any shade,
not the slim wax build staring at me
in the color crayon box who begs me to use him to color every inch of
    my family.

Nor is my hue mirror to the beautiful
that is our seceded lands, these reds
and browns mimic tones of old cherished
faces that my grandmother used
to mistake me for.

After four hours of listening to my dad
swear at a deck he was helping to remodel, I looked like the darkest
    and best parts
of a rainbow foods paper bag, filled
with delicious greasy fry bread. Put my arm up against the bag and
    disappear. Tell myself that I'm going to collect all
the used fry bread bags this summer to hide
behind, terrifying unsuspecting neighbors.

Naughty boy plans sizzle from the heat
coming off this khaki sack,
and it is the same as the bright yellow ball in the sky. Here is where I
    wonder why the sun is staying
like a relative who has nowhere in particular to go but doesn't wanna
    hear anymore love stories to my skin.

Inside the light of the Sun's happiest song,
I left that berated bit of wood and sat outside Dairy Queen and told
    anyone who would listen to the lie of my next life on the longest
    and most
Indigenous day ever.

CROSSROADS

Sometimes the lightning boy has to seal
the deal with the winning boy's magic.
Smokehouse Brown got to shake loose
and vibrate the brick and mortar
with ice water verse and hot
handed performance.

All of everytimes, you got to pull
the bended light from the room.
Push it into pulsing of your wrists.
Burn out all your fervor
with roar of *brun bête*.

How to Travel Home

At the bus stop between awake
and asleep, got asked where
I voted from. I told them
and the empty bedroom,
"I vote from my segment." Woke
up breathing fire from where
the champions live. Need to escape
but I only have gas money to make
it 1/3 of the way and I don't remember
the names of the churches my pop
used to work. Hopping from one
rectory to the next as we prayed
to brown relatives who prayed
to white imagination for a band
of angels coming forth to carry
us home.

Oceans of Time

How am I awake before
chain coffee house opens rusty
doors? Sit still in the empty
parking lot and hear him singing.

Pushes out a snagging song
to his wife Mary like her dress
isn't made from the first blanket
they shared. Laughs and talks
an "up before the sun" song
while cleaning his musket.

Laughs loud about misfires
and misadventures passing
us all by on a puff of roasted
coffee beans.

Forget I'm in the whip and nod
off for just a second. This is when
the hot dry day sneaks into my throat
and eyes. Who dreams of cold cups
of coffee, four-day-old pastries, and cute
plastic barista eyes?

Come to driving down a dirt road
I don't have any stories
about. Pull over just in time

to see earth reach up to sky
and give the gift of fire.

Feel lucky so take out my last
bit of braided sweet grass. Fire
to crackling scent of sugar
as earth, sky, birds and myself
sing in unison.

This choir on upcoming prairie fire
belts out a sure goot one. Sing
of wants and needs. Sing of pipes
and dreams. Sing of wanting to go
home so badly, that you would
shoot a ship's captain with a musket
just to feel the soft caressing arms
of a tiny woman who loves you beyond
your lovely and tragic stories.

MY GIRLFRIEND THINKS SHE'S HAN SOLO

At first I couldn't see the signs zipping past me like TIE fighters,
the LEGO Millennium Falcon,
her love of black vests,
a penchant for V-necks,
and a craze for utility belts and thigh holsters.

Shoulda known when
our second date was spent combing
toy store after toy store
looking for an exact replica of the
DL-44 heavy blaster pistol
in die-cast metal, not
"those stupid toys made of plastic."

Halloween parties, every year it's the same,
my chubby Wookie to
her short intergalactic smuggler.
The dark side of the force
blinded me to her delusion,
worried she'd leave me
cut up and left for dead
like so many frozen Tauntaun before me.

Nothing could damage how I feel about her though,
even when I say
I love you
and all I ever hear back is
I know.

Bannock Erotic

Lady, I will touch you with my mind.
Touch you and touch and touch
until you give
me suddenly a smile, shyly obscene.

Flour, yeast, sugar, veggie oil, water,
and powdered
milk, I will massage you with my hands.
Massage you and massage and deep fry
until you give
me suddenly a frybread, crisply obscene.

Bannock erotic —V. M. Cummings

SHE OF IMPLAUSIBLE TRIO

Rises the Sun
and Moon of me.
Makes the stars
come out in the night
of me.

Without her half-
full glass I'd dehydrate.

Wake before her and thank
everything that is for her.

Not for me,

for everyone she meets
becomes a retelling of her
brightness.

Brings out the warmth
in sub-zero me.

She brings me,
and I am grateful for our journey.

Something-est

Toughest Indian?
You wouldn't be the toughest Indian in the whole multiverse
if you were wearing your AIM windbreaker, red beanie, walkie-
talkie and carrying a mag light that had "toughie" scratched into it.

Might be the toughest Indian in your house when your mom
heads out, but hell, even the Smurfs had a tough Smurf. Even butter-
    flies
gotta be tough sometimes.

Now me? I'm no daisy. I'm no daisy at all.

You on the other hand, you're the 3 millionth toughest Indian, but ya
    only beat
out three dogs and four cats who just think they're Indian.
Growing up on the Rez and IHS
accepting their forged tribal IDs will do that to an animal.

If you tried to go into Canada right now the border cops
would confiscate you like you were a fantasy document.

Fiery faked fantasy documents of fierce fantasy Indians.

You wouldn't be the toughest Indian in the world if you had a teardrop
tattoo under your eye, a copy of Sherman Alexie's
book in your back pocket, and you were standing in front of the Lincoln
Memorial demanding that your treaty rights be taken seriously.

You're not even the toughest Indian with that outfit on.
Iron Eyes Cody is a tougher Indian
than you and Oscar de Corti ain't even Indian.
Winona Ryder is a way-ya-hey
tougher Indian than you, and her ma just stole
her name from an Indian princess some white people in Winona, MN,
made up.
Her ma musta heard the blue corn moon when she saw the name
displayed
in a store window. Yep, Ole Momma Ryder just walked in, shoved it in
her purse,
and left. Some traits are handed out like
American Indian College Fund
board appointments.

Embarrassing and hilarious all at the same time.

Video of Chicken Dance-Off Keeps Me Connected to Home

This here is pure vicious, every step.
A tussle so raw and uncontainable,
it was made illegal. In my heart
and brain, there is no other dance
fight that can compare, and none try.

You can't tally dedication to any wall
of champions, but you can see hours
spent to become better than legend.

Hands are sweaty watching
from the intertube. It's edge
of the couch cushion, and when I see
one rooster glide, no, shimmy sliiide,
to the end of the beat, I lose my savage
red mind ignobly.

Better than a movie action scene, battle
in an arena surrounded by relatives
named after leaders of retold glory.

In place of a heart, these two will rush
the gift through me just fine.

In the Shire of My Mind

Today has been an incredible rollercoaster.
My feet are frozen and tired from the weight
of it all. Imma slowly back into Bag End
on this side of things. Say things in private
to somewhere just left of center. Today's
long day of events have truly humbled me.
There is much to do and many to stand with.
If y'all need me I'll be posted up in the shire.
Frodo, Bilbo, and myself are gonna open
a pouch and send ships into circles.

What a day.

I Am Away

Root and stem small, frozen, and thawed,
out then back into deep freeze, pushes
out, face and hands reach up to nurse
obliged emission from on high.

This is our truest act, a blueprint we
search for with minds unfurled into a glimmer
and obscurity glazed in infinite midnight.

Gently, hold your palm to mine, share in my coy smile,
meet corneas at peak of almond tipped lid. We'll go round dancing all
    night, heads back, mouths open. At break of dark
blue and pitch of shaded envy, close your eyes,
turn your face to a horizon awash of blazed birth.

Reach and take shape of a tomorrow sustained
by the same flare that feeds and burns
with glory and chaos.

For My Valentine, on Our 8th Year

Thoughts of Megan are thoughts
of a great adventure.
Megan is one of the great ones,
a perfect match. An echo from the older
guys in my neighborhood floats
in, yelling at me to yell to her that
"she's your fit, tell her she's your fit!"
"Can't do it!" I yell back through time
to men frozen and armless, their jackets
now rock solid are carved to billow,
showing the movement of the wind
in winged history.

Carries me with a strength that hurriedly
pushes me down another bunny hole of memory.

Our first Valentine, nestled between bluffs
and river. The cake I made for her was done
while she was at class because sometimes
food is the only valentine I know.

A then future International Political Scientist,
hardly anything smoothed by her undetected.
Megan was then as she is now,
smart as a whip and sharp as a flint knife.

Had to enlist one of her tightest homegirls
because I knew, just knew that I wouldn't

be able to bake a cake *and* frost the thing
in the time it took her to walk two blocks to class,
discuss the issue of the day,
and come home.
Safaa Abdel-Magid, love you today and every day
for how much you helped to stretch out
the Megatron's walk home.

Even though I threw the frosting on *way*
before the cake cooled, this tiny bit of joy,
this woman who
raises the Moon in me
and puts the Sun in me to bed,
saw that melted mess, smiled, and read
the words aloud as if they had come
from her favorite book.

"Happy Valentines Megan."

This is when I learned how
"together forever and ever" felt.

In the quicksilver of her speaking
I saw a tiny bit of the universe
had broken off and come
to live in the earth lodge of my heart.

Into my lodge of lodges she brought an affection
that weighs more than 300 billion elephants.
With Megan goes my heart.

Attached my soul to hers with baling wire
and duct tape. Megan is my clearest forever
memory and with her, I climb mountains.

With a Megan, I begin to tackle every fear
and every bit of my own self-doubt.

With the sweet and kind gift of her
I make a potent love, a bond
that can never wash away.

Her and I, we make forever
in the sacred bundles
of our life together.

WIPED OUT

*Welcome, welcome. We're celebrating being wiped out by the
white man.*
—NORMAN BENSON

Lone Indian and Pilgrim celebrate
holiday with questionable roots.
No eye contact as the preparation
begins, would be best not invite
the guilt of the day to bubble up
too soon.

Cook with Incredible Indigenous
foods that the whole world
is now thankful for. The Pilgrim
says thank you, then adds another
buckle to clothes color of impure
carbon particles from incomplete
combustion of hydrocarbons.

Working in uneasy union to turn
food into other food with colors
that remind them of row upon
row of familiar warm twinkling
constellations. These two icons
of made up event smile and nod
at shared remembrances, begin
talk about their homelands.

Isolated Indian talks of where earth
meets sky, a region lush in devastating
bloom. Faint scent of honeycombed

cousin feral and dimly refined slowly
creeps in with silent but deadly
pungency.

Pilgrim says her lands are 80,000
cups of salty water away. Traveler
from hollow post comes from hard
wooden shoes and eternal battle
to take from the open hands
of water. These are territories
where theft dances with innovation.

Indian thinks about this place of windmills
and sore feet. Tries hard not to get his fear
sweat mixed into the creamed corn
and butternut squash.

They give thanks for continued survival
and after this feast; Pilgrim picks up a
musket and invites this Indian west.
Tells him that her Pilgrim god wants
only her to live in these, her new lands.

Onlyest Indian walks away empty-handed,
decides that he will celebrate with the water
next year, as their continued survival is now
too similar to be ignored.

Ride North on a Horse I Slicked Passed a Dim Electric Circus

Haggled the top hat and monocle
for two hours, made promises
for other trades and 8th horse-born
child, until the deal was whittled
down to a spit-filled handshake
that was dodged slimly with a quick
hair check.

For the right to rename this stallion
two things had to be left behind us
in the horizon. Saddle made of whiskers
from 33 bearded ladies so soft you fall
asleep midgallop. Wings made of duct
tape and fairytales span so wide
they hang shadows like Weeping Willows.

With our shared history tucked under arm,
a horse newly named Hickey and myself follow
a treasure map up past black bears, big otters,
and many other place markers named
after people we used to know.

5 Things I Learned in My First Poetry Mentorship Meeting

1. If you are a light-skinned native, you will be mistaken as white. If you are brown-skinned native, you will be mistaken for someone who works at the coffee shop in which you are meeting. In either case, be polite, and try not to stare down the menu items when talking about today's specials.

2. You will have a plethora of jobs, all of which will indirectly depend on your highly developed writing and reading skills. Most of these jobs will not be for pay, but when you do get paid, it will be because YOU'RE GODDAMN GOOD and said pay may be from a person from a family with lots money. That person may tell you after paying you that they will see to it that you never work in this town again; they may or may not be joking.

3. Walt Whitman and the many other notable white male poets had the same views toward you that you have toward them. Look past their race and gender and you will see someone struggling just as you do. Talk back to these poets through their own styles of poetry; it makes the poetry snobs cry.

4. Any poet can and will be your mentor. Look at their pieces and you will see them as they are through their writings. This will help you to understand them and maybe yourself.

5. Reverse mentorship is an important part of this process. Taking your mentor to exchange her 10-year-old cell phone that only works in speakerphone will be easy; it's getting 10 years of photos and memories off that cell phone that will be hard.

IN THE AMBER LIGHT OF MY AFTERNOON IMAGINATION

Barefoot, blending into the background like
so many bad Indians before me. I'm all Eyeballs
and full grin missing all kinds of scooped
and shovel-shaped teeth.
Talked three different pawnshops into taking 100
percent Indian teeth. With them bones I put
enough in the gas tank for a one-way ride back
up to bum tickers and a happy face full of gums
and PTSD that keeps me worried from not one, not two,
not three, not four, more than 500 miles away.
The bag I pack everything into is stuffed
with things in plastic bags. I wear ole timey
conductor's clothes and hatch an Indian
magician plan to get back Home. Paint myself
in a can of Deep Woods Off! and stand like Harry
Houdini on top of the new Break-up Bridge
and watch helpless as Indian man breaks up
with Indian Woman who breaks up with Indian
Woman who hurls obscenity and rage.
I'm on an oil tanker riding to somewhere familiar.
Careful not to spur 'em, I take my black dusty hat
off. Salute the Northside Natives who stand
and wave in the amber light of my afternoon
imagination.

BACK BEYOND THE DARK BLUES
OF REFLECTIVE SINGULARITY

With everyone midstride to choke
the horse of their lives, sometimes
I feel like single tree on the prairie
holding solid against wind's drill.

On this night of dawning catastrophe,
I am just back beyond the dark blues
of reflective singularity. Coming out
from somewhere to catch my weak
imminence, pour myself into old
form to keep measure of hardship
and harrowing hemic undertone.
Another of my arcane ambitions
climbs up from vault of past peril.

Dip myself in the memory of midnight
swim of Lake Nokomis. On first date
with aboriginal rapture, hedged my
bets on this dear woman's thirst
for adventure and myth of my young
legend. I was rewarded. Under radiant
moonlight, create contemporary ritual
between accidental touches and lies
we wanted to be real.

Stare into this doe-eyed dream. Wish
with my beaten heart to materialize
her as she was, in lake, under full moon,
holding me in ruined embrace.

TIME TRAVEL

Turned around and saw my shadow penguin slide
into the bathroom.

Threw once cooked bacon grease,
Mazola corn oil, and oil from the pan
from the last time my Gramma Blanche
ever made fry bread in the spaces
between me and the commode.

Threw off my horn rims, and slid head first
into the possible.

Found the path back Home on three types
of deadly crude, not counting the ones
that slosh in metal moving barrel. Honey-
colored madness sings me an old-time
Jackie Bird song as charcoal-hued revenge
contaminates and spreads.

"You're not one, You're not two, you're not three,
you're not four, you're 500 miles, away from home."

The whole Bird band plays then echoes back
into the vault of my mind.

Wish for tape one last time while collecting earth's twisted
Amniotic fluid for tomorrow's rebirth ritual.

GREATEST CONTEST POW-WOW IN THE WHIRL

Snow heard Thunder singing loud
so Lightning was asked to round dance.

Wish it would never stop.
Wish the only thing that could
stop it would be the most humid
heat of Minnesota, or floods.
Much water to wash away control
and cleanse the oak barrel.

The Seasons,
when they meet to share their balance
isn't like silent snowflake dance
through the park. When Seasons
touch, they remember powerful
end and celebrate explosive rebirth.
It's like the finals at the greatest
contest Pow-Wow in the whirl.

Cousins of Bear and Mountain Lion,
relatives to Eagle and Wolf.
Seasons are untamable forces
and when they meet to celebrate
their ancestors, my marrow begins
to vibrate all three of my major
macromolecules.

HEAD COLD REACTION

Feel like my head has been soaked
in deer brain and stretched tightly
in my mom and dad's garage for winter,
to be safely kept.

Kept the cough and wheeze song
up all night, 98 pushups
and only my fat-encrusted lamb
heart keeps time. My heart
and mocs are on the side of the bed,
alpaca-stuffed for speed not for comfort.

Comfort isn't easy to come by.
Been to the bathroom more times
than I care to admit. Not ashamed
of the frequency, worried I've grown
attached to the space.

Space and time, two things
that are hard to come by in city
life. To patient zero in the zombpocalypse,
these become weapons, would only take hours
to infect the miniest of apples.
How does that make you feel?

DREAM

Was making my way around the city
and realized that no one
had a face. The backs of everyone's
head just went all the way
around. People were talking
and talking, but it was coming out
from hairstyles. Ponytails were telling
me things, grown-out buzz cuts
were saying hi, and I recognized
everyone. Didn't actively pay attention
to what the backs of heads look like,
but everyone was there. Relatives
of Cousin It move around in my glitch-
filled brain, afterthoughts wait to visit
me in my dreams.

THE ONLY PERMANENCE I'LL EVER NEED

Time again to check and recheck life systems of support. Put on suit of space polymers and check crumbling bridge of interpersonal relation-ships. Count fingers, toes, and tragedies. If any list comes up with more in the plus column than before, seek appropriate medicinal ritual or ceremonies at your disposal.

Oxygen at normal.

Stress at normal.

Rocket of inward descent is being ridden down to unknown speeds. While others brace for impact, you, shining, gleaming like a high school piece, you had to hold down cause the block is always at volcano level, you breathe, turn off the autopilot, hit the reverse thrusters, then kick, and coast. Metallic taste won't go walk away from your mouth as easily as you did from that crash, but there are always new adventures down the road, and the story, it's the only permanence I'll ever need.

THE SWEET SCIENCE OF HABITAT

The wind is a bully. I'm inside painting, where my
paintbrushes are bullying around some paint on the canvas.
—BUNKY ECHO-HAWK

Wind pushes me,
can't push back, swing
wild and grab at fistfuls
of nothing as wind does
nothing but push me
harder.

Tired arms and legs shake
at the defeat from invisible
force. Withered and dry
from endless fight, tumble
away to fight another way.

Water drowns me,
can't smother back, flail
with panic while lungs slowly fill
with the blue-green abyss.
Water does nothing but fill
a me shaped container.

Heavy with the language
of the water people.
Greeted respectfully when
finally touch sandy silt bottom.

Earth shakes and swallows
me whole but cannot

reach out from beyond
muddy containment to
consume it all.

Spins me to unknown parts
of the not known, can do
nothing, no thing, but free fall

like everyone else.

Terraforming the Final Frontier

Christ, I need a spaceship now. That's not a prayer to Jesus, so it doesn't count, Gramma. Not looking for a small city floating in space going where no perm has gone before. Just need a ship that can cruise between all the planets with enough trunk space to hold some 16s, a digital amp, and some mining gear. The plan isn't to just get a ship and dip. Leaving all y'all as a blip on my nav screen isn't how it's going down. No, gonna mine all the rocks round dancing around Earth. Become the first trillionaire or fofillianaire and get my ass to Mars. Then, then I'll leave all y'all flapping on this decaying giant marble. Nobody will miss a spec of brown sand zipping away in a spaceship on the river of my imagination.

FROM THE UPPER PILOTHOUSE

I live
on a tugboat.

It isn't sinking.
We
are not falling.

This ship is slowly
being accepted back
into murky muddy depth.

This isn't a story.
We
are not singing glory.

I live
on a horse,

who is in the slowest suicide
race ever.

THE BEAR NAILS ARE COMING IN DIFFERENT

Jesus and his uncle the Devil hang from one
chain in my bedroom. Naked, smell
of six-hour car ride and night spent full
of worry, sweat, and a rotisserie-style
toss on a couch with ghost legs.

Lay my forearms in between the rungs
of the radiator in our bedroom, bow
my forehead and begin to pray
like my uncle asked me to do.

Pray before the metal idols of good
and evil that take no inventory
of my soul. Notice my feet and the weird
curl on one of my big toes, the bear
nails are coming in different.

Flatter and with no point, these quarter-
inch thick daggers pushing out past my fat
feet mimic my strength today.

Realize that I am doing everything but pray
and have said none of the prayers
learned as a Spark in Awanas. Today,
after a full day of the spin and move, humble
myself and beg and beg for my ancestors to rise
up out of history and their watery crypts.

In a tiny corner of the universe, a powerless
Me looks blindly into brown sadness-soaked
arms and beg and plead for more water, for
skies to burn gray and loud with thunder
to cleanse my family.

GET BACK HOME

We just want to come home, just want to know how to get
back to your home, Junior.
—JUNIOR KIMBROUGH, "ALL NIGHT LONG"

Turned off the phone but it doesn't stop
an echo from my past from calling at two
in the morning. Says no thing directly,
maybe just wants to remember when we
raced fast and free on ponies
made of fiberglass and parental permission.

Other waves in the water of history fight
for phone time, splash and slur on a connection
that is slowly cutting in and out. Can hear the click
clack of bar doors closing for the night. Voices
swim out of muddy water, no longer bounce off
of sweaty wall and dropped ceiling.

These remembered tones twinkle by yellow-colored
streetlight; laugh at the white noise filling
up the space in between the parking lot pimps
and the others who feed on the hustle. With Q-tips
for teeth and mouth made of cotton candy, these soft
soft verses sing.

Lost, She Moved

Twenty years out from first flight, she is beaten,
homeless in a tent on lone prairie. Messages
sent out on an even-tempered summer day ask
for small money, a neat fix.

Fire that she once carried, magically taken
from hands made of tarred steel. Her incalculable
gift, buried in mud and muck now. Twists
and spins at bottom of lake that binds
her ancestors who can only wonder
with everyone else when the next one
will come Home.

She, now a cutout on a billboard passed
on freeway screams. Do not follow her down
broken endless plight. Shouts to me every day
I pass her to remember her strong, dancing
to the heartbeat of the people
full of confidence and promise.

Indian Jesus

I am hunting again, you
are not safe.

My last homeboy on the big
side wakes me with promise
of foolproof food. Asks me
again if he'll be ok. Lights
a bad one to burn down.
Coughs and passes backward
to the picture of his ancestors.
They huff and all balls roll
in my direction. Bootlegger
stops by, asks me if he'll
stop killing everyone before
someone comes to make
the dirty poison from his blood.
They begin to tell the story
of us. How they found me,
the state in which they
came by me. Barefoot
in the Roach with tank top
and cargo pants, my Phillips
uniform with my socks rolled
over a gold buck knife.

In a park that no one goes
into during the dark. A fish
and a stone rolled a long

and dirty tale. Said they heard
an old story had setup
on the court and was hitting
fifty-foot jumpers while telling
everyone their future. They hit
the park as fast as knobby
cinnamon roll knees could carry
them and found the line wrapping
around The Peacemaker Center
as if it still stood. As if the slime
and gangrene still held it all
in place. In the spot where
Buckanaga's stolen ring once
stood, Walleye and Pipestone
carried me away to animal-
infested hideaway. Told me
to sleep, that Rest would lie
down at my right and the shine
of what will never be will inch
up from the drains and whisper
indecent plan.

I do not know what day it is,
you will not be able to hide
from me.

On a day like today, I opened rickety
white porch door to see the bounty
left in the name of wonder. Boxes
of doughnuts, deer jerky, beadwork,
Jo-jos, and whole roasted chickens.
All these gifts with tiny rolled-up
questions and statements attached
like pouches of that sweet Nokomis
blend I only smoke when I feel
literary.

"Will I ever get out of here?" "Does
my husband still love me?" Are you
here to save us?" "Will they hoe me
out for rent money?" Questions stuck
to food stuck to me stuck to every single
cabinet in the place to be.

Boulder after boulder, he ties them all
in a Duluth pack, packing each one
with more care than they deserve.
The truth has been brushed
from his wicked tongue and dream
of tomorrow has been scaled away
from black and curly hair. This Indian
Jesus has no more answers to give.
He has on twice resurrected Air Jordans
and has taped one last truth to his body
as he leaves them flappin' and stompin'.

There is nothing more to offer up
to you. Save yourself.

THE OLD AGE HOME OF STEREOTYPES

Seeking conclusion to ignoble savagery,
the decapitated heads of Indigenous
men are an aged stoic tragedy.
Let them be retired.

Buxom subservient maidens kneel to the wonder of marketing.
Memories in perpetual perdition, these are
great-grandmothers to
the ironic women in Hipster Headdress.
Part of the female gender
still chained in an antiquated
sphere pushed by an undead Sarah Hale.
Unwanted, indirect wave of female sexuality directly placed onto half
        a race
of kidnapped invisibility. A human rights crisis, 10 times the national
        average,
Native women are dancing on to the jingles
of inauthentic leather clad, cherry-skinned dolls. These forgotten war-
        riors of suffrage, brown hues on the battlefield of bleached desire
        fight against assault rates that rival sexual violence in war zones.

Everything and anything that continues
to depict any race of people
as uncanny variants,
Little Black Sambo
Frito Bandito
Chief Wahoo
Cartoonish crimes that end in "O."

Say these names and let dams break from their use, and then
let them all set quietly into gray regretful misery.
let them walk each other swiftly to the
old age home of stereotypes.

Hang up our imposed titles of Product and Logo. Let another race
    strong enough to bear the weight of this marketed oppression
    take up the mantle. Let a race full in culture and pride take on
    places like Urban Outfitters and Paul Frank Industries when they
    redefine what derogatory and honored means.

Let my eyes never again see the Land O'Lakes princess or any of her
    horrible brothers and sisters. Rot, cigar store Indian,
rot and begin to erode away.
Let them all wither and retire into history.
Let them die a good death.
Let me sing their death song.
Let them fade into a narrative
that we helped to change.
Let us look back at what was
and be reminded of what could be
if we didn't fight for us.

An Unedited Round Dance Song Named "Chubby Brown Man's Choice in the Pow Wow of My Heart"

Saw a picture today on one
of many social networks
I swim in, and in that instant,
as I scrolled past it, a whole
poem I have been trying
to word since my last joe job
wrote itself.

Image projected in my dome
with the phrase "oh you wrong
for that" seared itself into my
eyes. Currently it is this chubby
brown man's choice
in the pow wow of my heart,
and I am round dancing
this sentiment past
the crabs in the barrel up above
this whole state, past this country
even.

Before I tell a personal
hero to discreetly kiss my rear,
right in the crack, I do a lap around
the airspace of this country's capital
and wave goodbye as I head to my
base on the moon.

They wrong for That and a whole lot
more, and now finally after much talk,
much deliberation, I have a shaft
straightener for my traditional Indin
literary arrow construction.
Write this before you lose it forever,
all your love, all your hate.

Man of Wood's Lodge

On an adventure to see the stolen landmarks
of the most wiped out of the last human
beings. We rode up and down the lands
of the people of the first light, and my eyes
were filled, emptied, and refilled.

It was during these travels that I met an old
white man who cut the natural circles of trees
into cold squares that reminded me of tombstones.
Here on the East Coast where this man in a bubble
who doesn't know anything about his own religion,
told me over and over to put aspects of my race's
spirituality into a play.

From what chair of authority does any white male
speak to tell an Indigenous person that their sacred
is only on par with guys and dolls and other fakery
from a stage. His mouth was made of foul river
with ears made of two tightly closed stone doors.
Could not reach this tired old programmer
from the first matrix as he was only able to see race
as a luxury that others deal with or ruin art with.

Left him astonished in his tomb of beautiful colors
and square pegs from the circular world. One day
he will wipe the privilege from youthful eyes
that tell 1,000 stories, but it will be too late. Man of
wood will understand the words to my song
only when his last sun has set.

NEW MIGRATION RITUAL

Shimmy slid to the gulf
with a summer's worth
of collected jellyfish, conchs,
and whelks. Made 521 years
of treaties and promises
to a school bus driver
for the ride south.

Kept her awake with stories
about sea turtle earth lodges
and coastal plains made of two
kinds of forever with the bluest
greens that can only be seen
from my tribe's ancestral village
on the Moon.

Zigged when she zagged
a massive alligator wrestler
named The Chub. Patted The
Chub where his toe-shaped
head connected to his rectangle
of a body and dipped like a dirt
road leading to a boat dock.

Hitched a ride with America's
only circus clown biker gang.
Traded these painted-up people

a mixture made of cayenne pepper
and dried sweat from a gator
wrassler. Blended in bus station
bathroom, trafficked some of that old
time ancient Indian flimflam.

Clinch this deal using my best
vanishing movie Indian
voice. "When peacock of self-
doubt rises, rub this dub all
over yourselves while loudly
chanting praises for these secret
and sacred Indigenous ingredients."

Took these undercover plastic
shamans for every single one
of their poodle-shaped balloons
and ink-spitting flowers. Pointed
them towards a secret golden
road whose path starts just behind
a building that doesn't exist.

Could have hustled them
with their stereotypes of me for
years but had come instead to humid
end. The point of return was so far
behind it was almost back
in front of me. Waited four days
on sandy white beaches
until a Leatherback the size
of a smart car swam up
to make epic trade.

After going over all of my tricks
and treats he accepted every

last bit of it for his home
made of origin and evolution.
Lathered myself in bacon grease,
slid into hard-shelled womb.
Looked out to the line made of water
and oxygen, plugged my nose,
and dove in face-first. Out and out
past ocean liner and three-story waves.
Flipped over and backstroked
into the calm and silence
of my new ceremony.

THE POWER OF WHITE

Hey I believe Indians and Wasicus
don't belong together. ever. as well.

but I can't seem to shake the tiny
white woman who just loves the shit
outta me.

I mean just that deep down agape
love that can only come from someone
whose race blatantly tried to wipe
my race the fuck off
the face of turtle island.

My love for her pierces my heart
like justified arrows into her ancestors.
I just wanna love her so much,
her grandmas and grandpas on both
sides of her stink Wasicu family disown
her and take away the trillions they
literally and theoretically took from me.

I wanna love her so hard her white
guilt pops outta her like the packets
of mayo she's constantly trying to get
me to try. I wanna love her enough
to tell her that I've tried mayo before
and that shit tastes gross and unfamiliar,
like our love.

I wanna love her so much that by sheer
osmosis her Wasicu family understands
that I never want to be friends on Facebook
or any other network, real or imagined.

I wanna love her so hard that it breaks off
and my dad takes into the garage to fix it
but when he comes out it doesn't fit
anymore and now it kinda wobbles on
flat services.

I wanna love her with so much magic
that every Wasicu who dresses
up as an Indian for Halloween is immediately
transformed into a wooden cigar store Indian,

and then,

I wanna douse myself in kerosene and light my love on fire!

Fast Horse

A man moves and pushes these new chairs
around like he just put in a new battery.
Fumble with mics because, really, to watch
him go is a better story. Swift, slender
as mic stand, he is much like *The Littles*
on Saturday. Spins with purpose, like lights
are about to go out any second and his
escape plan is just a stage whisper
away. He moves with happiness,
like he is thinking about his relatives who
live happy between the walls. I break away
and check mics, check for Wi-Fi,
for signal to send a signal.
Find my pop's name in the list of networks
just smiling at me.
Sit and remember when things were more
checkers than chess. Think of his elderly
gentleness. Sit and sing his name quietly
under the hum of security-system fan.
Phonetically as if I have just landed
in his encampment and he has taken pity
on me.
"Ta-shunk-a Loo-sah, Ta-shunk-a Loo-sah,"
Fast Horse.
Say his name louder and wonder at the brick
wall if I will find happy step. Look up and ask
exposed ceiling joists if I too will find marinated
calm after youthful storm and rage of everyday
forecast.

Deep in the count of wintered lives, I try
to remember all the words and phrases
learned from him. They are in a book
on a top shelf while I dangle in our memory,
arms stretched out to the nothingness.
Pull out a time he tuned up some fool who
lost his way onto the wrong porch. He
and downstairs neighbor Peanut laugh
after they help him up. Tease as scavengers
slink out to help themselves to the contents
of this mystery's wallet, "Where's Tonto, and why
the hell didn't you listen to that skinny handsome
Indin?"
We pack, keep it moving toward a powwow
highway just past crumbled bridge of yesterday
Indians.

CELEBRATION OF STILLNESS IN THE SHARK'S HEART

Watch as trees stop their dance.
Car motors seize and become
motionless. A man in the park who hunts
for buried treasure falls over.

For thirty whole seconds,
world that swims around me
quits being us. Maybe we noticed
each other. Taken in by sweetness,
moment that never stays
long. Saw each other as friends
once before a rush swept over
the beach of a brief connected
happiness.

Wave goodbye starts a domino
effect. Moment into moment
becomes birth coming
to the end.

Will try the next four lifetimes
to stop, seize up the machine
again. Man who searches
for all that glitters brushes
off his antique machine, begins
his shuffle anew. The trees
go-go dance to songs only the birds know.

BEEN THINKING ABOUT IT FOREVER

The tense and tender of muscles
telling me to go home. After today
it's obvious that the hustle
and bustle has eaten its fill,
and me? I feel emptied
from the meal.

The smartphone of my mind
needs a recharging, so I'm heading
to where the earth meets the sky
and then perhaps other adventures
and more stories.

Call to myself and in response can
only hear a whisper down a hallway
underneath an ancient roar
that today was quelled by the voice
of thin uncontaminated bravery.

My balance is off and it's time to go
home. I'll be out for a while, have
to see it, feel it, and know it, need
to refocus, need to close my eyes
and feel the season change against
my face, need something that's always,
always, just out of arm's reach.

POLLEN TAKERS' RETURN

Last bumblebee in the world droops
clear wings on my window sill, asks
me if I know how to really listen. Cut
open a slim cowboy killer, put one parts
sugar four parts into my favorite coffee
cup. Edge my opening offer up close
to this buzzing relative and
whisper, "story."

Out of long spindly tongue twists saga
of a kingdom so grand it is sewn
into the beating heart of Earth. Lone
bumblebee tells of kinship
to the Sun. Begins secret dance
that binds both together in warmth
and survival.

Sings a song about the flower's electromagnetic
rapture for all bumble tribe. Chants
about lonely wait for the pollen takers'
return.

Pushes the cup away, tells me
it is enough for now. Climbs up to my
Mandan earlobes and thanks them
personally for accepting today's retelling.
Dances out of my window into desolate

drone apocalypse, does one lap around
my house before disappearing into the
midafternoon flare.

Dancing and Singing Moon to Bed and Sun to Birth

Up before the sun to do my
1-2 thing in the park. It's cold
as a witch's you know what,
and the passing nursing students
must think I'm just another
regular crazy. I am, but sometimes
this place calls to me just before
sunlight spreads over this tiny
neighborhood like butter
to bread. Sliced by heavy gray
concrete, dirty brown ice water,
and the hope of fixing a shattered
youth, this slice that is no longer
called The Murder.

My hood that's no longer
a hood is being run by 2nd
and 3rd ringers who understand
the gentrification and invite
its style into the foundation
and architecture. Even the last
Indian gang, 7th Generation Naturals,
fronted by a red-headed suburbanite
that I beat in a game of 21 in a backyard
one icy early morning just like this one.

More meat for the grinder, more stats
that need counting. Press my hands down

past the icy snow and deep into the frozen
brown skin of my mother, pray, rinse,
and repeat.

Here in the middle, here in this in-between
of darkest night and brightest day begin
to create something that hasn't been seen
here for hundreds of years.

There I create new world medicine from old
world pain. Dancing and singing Moon
to bed and Sun to birth. Convulse and wail
in the park with muddy hands as the 2500th
annual Crow Pow Wow carries on over my head.

My magic's drained away again into another new
day, hidden in a park, tucked away from everything
by bird squawking and river flowing. One new ritual,
one less spot of light dancing in moonlit misery.

BiG Word Mom Lets Me Tag Along

Knows I'm excited, asks me if the ability
to contain myself is in there, somewhere.
With a grin bigger than a Wonderland
cat, I say "of course."

We walk to parts unknown past doors
and gates that look like my aunts
and uncles. Hop step through secret
passageway and known hallway.
Up 17 flights of stairs and only go down
three. Pass by murals as big as mountains
and sidewalk chalk designs longer
than time.

We are on an epic journey and BiG word
Mom just keeps walking by it all, humming
the same 49 while her beaded bandolier
bag dancing to the rhythm of her swaying hips.

After we passed the second herd of roaming
bison, and just before I decide never to go walk
about again we come upon a medium-sized
building with a giant-sized Panda working
the front door. To get in, BWM tells me everyone
has to tell a good poem.

Watch as BWM walks up, gives one eyebrow raise
at the cow-colored porter and is let in without word

one. Try to smooth in behind her but Cat-foot
ain't having it, and clicks the velvet rope closed.

BiG Word Mom says, "Hurry June bugg, much leaves
to eat." Around a corner she zips, leaving me
and the cuddliest monster alone.

Sweat starts listening to the self-doubt bouncing
around my squash, and the dam breaks just beyond
my hairline. Fumble through poems but am sure none
of them are good enough. Tell myself that this doorman
probably has a master's in creative writing, meets up
with the most epic of writing group partners,
and has even guest edited *Magical Animal Review*.
Wonder what torture awaits me if I don't it get down
with the get down quick.

Turn everything off, close my eyes, and tell about
the first Panda that moved into my neighborhood.
In a tree on The Ave. outside the library, a Panda
called Jerry sat easy and ate pawfulls of Jerky.
Sprouts of bamboo are pushed away, tells us all
that he will never go back, give him the fastest fried
food and let him eat it by the blue light of broadcast
TV. Jerry has divorced life of rock and tree, tells us
that he will walk into the horizon of irradiated future,
and he will leave his old life to new wonder.

Then overwhelmed, I tell it all, push the highs
and lows, tell of victories and defeats. Sneak
in the everyday dance of trying to make it out
of one tree in to the next. Pull off magic stuck
to my teeth and make it sing the glory.

Open my eyes and this whole damn place
is so still I can hear air leaving lungs. BiG Word
Mom is standing in front of me, arms crossed,
smile on her face. When I ask where the Panda
went, BWM laughs loud and says, "That old black
and white bruiser went outside to reevaluate its
life, now c'mon fool boy there is much to see
and only enough eyes to miss the good stuff."

Lamb Hearts

Forget the suburban rings, carrot
of homogenized living amongst
people who lost their clans,
their connection, and the way.
Forget the well-to-do neighborhoods,
and their fast and loose understanding
of together. Forget these herds who
have forever robed themselves
in words of the people while
their stampedes crush and maim
the very lives they pretend to hold
with velvet limb.
Their tactics are always rolled out
from 50-year-old carbons. New
saviors riding on raggedy chariots.
Using the word community as kindling
for their own fires while my hood,
burns and burns the same blue hue
it always has.
I will continue to make pleasant
recollection here in the Southside.
Let me spin without charge between
stuccoed streets ample with elegance
and range. From these passages
I make distinct dynasty with people
filled with stories of jubilance
and jilted catastrophe. I will share
my count with homes inside revision

where historic matchstick men began
claims to earth and river that still do
not belong to them.

60 Seconds That Never Was

The sun, setting,
shining through
the branches of the trees
at the end of winter.

Will you call me this
when I'm so old
that my feet no longer
touch the floor?

When what's left of my diabetic
soul is too honeyed to cut
with lemon and tea.
Will you call to me in my
language and whisper
sweetly to me when
I'm crying in the shower
over something I saw
on a late-night infomercial
that reminded me of Stephanie May
and Stacy Ann?

Will you tell me stories
like when I was a young guy,
hands on face, staring
into the night
and our Anoka apartment ceiling?

Will you remember to call
me husband when you
are too old to remember
who I am? Will you tell me
I'm handsome after they
amputate both of my legs?

Will we call to each other
in the night, during the day
when all that's left of each of us
is a shadow on the picnic table?

Star Chart

"The block is the smallest
universe amongst the larger,
more well-known universes."

Our intergalactic ambassadors
wait on either side of our corridor.
Asking you to change, one cardboard
sign at a time.

This block that's yours
and mine was featured
on *National Geographic* in the '70s,
our seceded mindset
was followed by the best
trackers in all of Nat Geo,

from our rise to trip and fall,
they been archiving our ebb
while our flow
goes and goes
on down the muddy Mississippi.

This block was ground zero
when they put all the match
sticks together and tried
to break them all.

This block is where we learned
"one Indin weak, many Indin Strong

and since then?

It's been on and on
till the break break of Dawn"

FATA MORGANA

In response to Jonathan Thunder's The Beautiful Light of Delirium Tremens

Three days after the last angry laugh
and now there is much whispered
praying on the other side of another locked
door. Crackerjack Rose has slipped
by me once again and is sharing
his visions with everyone who cannot shake
the Thirst. Pray for us and see us all
past images we beg not to see.

The fulgent fuchsia false prophet leaps
from Saturday morning adventures to conceal
an aged, undoubted kismet in the gleam
of his robe. At first he appears as happy
delusion, draped in the regalia of his Disney
brethren, butterfly stroking magically around
the soaked heads of future betrayal.
He has helped many after making sweaty,
salty mistakes.

As Old Scratch c-walks in the corner
to songs from your high school jeopardy.
The blue devils slowly slip snakes
into your slick kicks. You dance and shake
with newfound confidence to a beat
old, but new to you. The coral pachyderm
you call Uncle patiently waits for his time
to dance you backward, away
from the intersection of your most well-kept
enshrinement.

Delirium Tremens sings as an echo, whispers
sick salty dreams of horror into a quantum
singularity, stretched with the shadow
of our history. The last door has opened.
Steam from another waking stage
four terror has risen away. Clutching the first grasp
of a newborn sanity, openly,
we roar into a starless night lit imperfectly
by our remission. How can such agonizing
aftermath blind with such velvet and salmon-
colored light?

The Sacred Convergence

On a red and white painted-up pony, an old hustler from White Earth scoops me. He's a grizzly one for sure, and before we can make eye contact he asks me what Rez I'm from. "The sacred convergence, only get one of you every other year, hop on." So we ride, the last two Indians in all the galaxy, riding out on flame and freeze. The pow wow of the iron giants waits for us all always; its line in the sky matches my heartbeat. Pushing past rubber and steel stampedes, we make haste to the center of everything. We are like every other Indian though, late to save the day by 512 years. So we drop these racist tonto headbands from sweaty brows and walk empty-handed into the next story.

Day in sun.
My skin, dark brown paper bag
after it has been filled with just-made
fry bread. Skin tone of the gods
as I sing the Sun to rest.

ATEWAYE KI (MY FATHER)

I know you're six-by-eight Pa, but this morning around 5:30, I heard you laugh and then I smelled your smell. Fresh cut wood, Marlboro Red 100s ("Remember in the box, junior"), and that salty sweat from living a life filled with a struggle that would slowly take away your legs and vision.

As I crept outta bed to burn the sage and pray, the way you showed me to pray ("Waska, it's just like making a phone call to the great mystery") I thought about when I went to your sculpture in South St. Paul this last time I was in town. Geez, they take care of it like they dreamed and cut it themselves; you'd be happy.

Uncle Neil called and said Uncle Tony danced on, but in the shadow of that conversation I was only be able to picture you and me going to visit Uncle Tony and staying the night at his place in the Y. Then later to when we would visit his shop in Duluth, where I would first notice that you share the same smile lines, hairlines, and laugh. That same laugh that would echo through my house early this morning.

Old, good memories who will round dance the new painful ones into my mind and Mind.

Pa, I can't find the strength to come and bring this news to you. I can't find the will to see you without the power you've cultivated in me. For the shame it brings me not to tell you, to not have you help me hold up this sadness and sacredness, I am sorry.

I'm pulled out of this Rez car of emotion because I know that I can look ahead to hear us laughing, talking, teasing, and healing each other.

LERLEANE

To the midnight blue automobile
I nicknamed Lerleane, with doors
made from permanent solution
to lifelong problem.

I do not dream of you.

Your chrome bumper winked
at me while I was on the bus
to my second job, and I hatched
half-baked plan to become
your lord.

To the lightest bit of soul I had left,
traded for a bag of nightmares
and a trunk that would hold hand-
made speaker box, digital capacitor,
two amplifiers, and a nickel-plated bit
of terror.

I did not come by you on the up
and up.

To the winter I slept huddled
in your front and back seats
while something I made
with knowledge stolen

from the library trickle
charged your dying heart.

I do not sit on three-season porch,
gaze into shimmer of your dark
infinite skin tone and reminisce
our faded history.

To your new owner who bought
you at auction. I am not sorry
for carving my true name
in the glove compartment,
on the metal under the driver's seat,
and on all four wheel wells.

To hell with you and my stolen horse
you ride in on.

Two Extra Arms and Legs

Dreamed of office work again,
dealt death in 1s and 0s.
None push paperwork death
like me. Swam in intertubes
of plumbing like I was
trying to save a 64-bit
princess with 8 bits of honor.

The four extra limbs really made
sense in a half-awake-half-asleep
kinda way. Spent all my
seclusion in the passenger seat
of the Batmobile. Clutch seatbelt
and wish for quieter moments
as the pedestrians, bikers,
and other drivers gave us
the Pristine Salute.

Yellow tights and green-scale
panties was busy. Big Pointy lets
her do this "like all the time"
she said as she paid more attention
to my emotions than the road. I look
at the speedometer and wonder
if we are really about to smash
the land speed barrier.

Drew diagrams on the ransom note
this woman of bat would leave
for my loved ones. Nothing
practical, just wishes in graphite
and ink stuck in between glue and
glossy cut-out magazine alphabet.

Maybe if I can wake up this time.
If I shake loose from these paper
clipped bindings, I can get my
friend J. Dangerously to graft
me some Otto Octavius type
of tendrils.

SAVAGE SOMETHING

Sometimes I take these brown and gold
glasses off. Look past folds of fat
on my body and see the steroid-
pumped stereotype of myself. He
is a masterpiece.

Tucked in between pictures of lowriders
and paper-thin models, his reddish
glow catches anyone who passes by.

Winks at me while confidently clutches
another of his ivory captives. These pink
and writhing people are helpless to escape
perfectly defined muscle filled with the
hot air of appropriation.

Faux prisoners caught behind bars of wild
straight black hair lean in and away. Loving
and loathing this savage something.

Put my glasses back on and rebraid my
fuzzy curly hair. Spend the afternoon
in front of the mirror posing and worried
that buried deep inside me is a grocery
store romance Indian just waiting
to come out.

Unfadeable, So Please Don't Try to Fade This

I am uncontainable
Like Stephanie
Stacy
Angel
Cheryl
and Blanche
like Bensons, No one can hold me down,
But many try.

I am controllable season
Like winter
Summer
Spring
Fall
like weather, No one can tell me when to be me,
But many try.

I am unstoppable force
Like Water
Fire
Ground quake
like Earth, No one wants me running free,
But some try.

One Last Neon Buffalo Jump

Tonight, stood on the wall
at the top of the world.
Looked out at the crumble
and change of the downtown
skyline, and yelled into the haze
that floats above those chained
Iron Giants.

Our echo returned with the winter
count of wild Indian boys. We
converged at Survival's spear tip
for one last neon buffalo jump
where river's edge used to sing
our names.

At thin edge of colonial singularity
we wrap ourselves in connected story,
pass memory around the circle in a metal
coffee cup meant for campfires
and marshmallows.

This evening, just for a tiny bit, we
take turns dipping this makeshift ladle
in the fountain of our youth, laugh
at the old men we slowly become.

GREATEST INDIAN WOMAN IN THE WORLD CONVENTION

Today when I pulled up
to 35th and Bloomington
you looked like all the best
summers I've ever lived.

Before I knew it was you,
I knew it was a you
that would and did steal
my breath away under
shaded tree.

On this busy corner deep
in the Southside of things
I saw a life worth leaving
my own for.

Saw beautiful almond-
shaped eyes that bring
out the Indian in me
every time I stare in to them.

This is the way it has been
since I first looked into them
as young urban brave wishing
he could count coup to earn
a name he will never hear
you say.

In the moments between
breath and breathing I saw
a good and hard future filled
with struggle and support
as I grew into the man I passed
by 500 years ago.

Then, the light turns green,
and I smile and tease
at the possibility hanging
in the air above me.

A Poem for Mr. J

A poem is a city at war.
—Charles Bukowski

A poem is an old drunk pretending to be another drunk while looking out into a city that hates and fears it. A poem is Batman and every last one of the X-Men all in one nasty, three-clawed, bataranged pull. A poem is spraying aqua net into three pieces of bread that sit over a glass jar as a filter. A poem is the Cherry Kool-Aid you mix into your filtered hairspray underneath the franklin bridge at a place where only the buffalo roam. A poem is wanting what no one will give you. A poem is the sickest and depraved archnemesis who flip marked coins to tell your future and release nerve gas to put a smile on your face. A poem is the last phone call from the newest center of your universe, who tells you to put down that jug and pick up a paintbrush. A poem is the blood that flows through my veins, pulses out to leave a trail back to my wicked history. A poem, my friend, you have no idea what a poem is, but you're caged in one of the most epic I've ever read.

Cease

Slip past unsuspecting blue orb round
dancing across the sky. Make my way
to the foot of BiG Word Ma's
mountain. It has been over 300 Hollywood
Indian moons since last I made this trek
to give thanks to the architect of my
concepts. Embarrassed I climb, long
since I bowed my head in humility
and offered up my shine.

The path shifts in a night darker
than boiled owl. Stop to close my eyes
and listen for crooked cracked branch
while wondering if I'll ever see BiG Word
Ma's porch again. When I open my eyes,
the glow from the Sun climbing up the
other side mountain is filling in all the best
places, and I can see a sign posted to a tree.

"BWM is on sabbatical, take your silly bottoms
back down her mountain, all requests handled
on a trial by fire basis. Boy, if you are reading this,
I have taken a hot air balloon ride around the whirl,
don't know when I'll be back again. Hang tough
and make your way back in the same time
it takes a cereal company to mail decoder rings.
—BWM"

As I take my silly bottom back down, chuckle
at the thought of a world holder taking time out
to talk Time off the razor's edge. Even BiG Mas
need time away from the constant ebb and flow
of our soft destruction.

Death of Steel and Stone

Stopped singing to my shoes
today. My winged tennies stopped
their dance the same day flame
spit and cursed a new hole in the earth.

In a story older than any 40-acre
allotment, the Moon, filled with loss,
sung to mocs quilted of cougar
and buckskin asking them to help
reunite him with his family.

It was a hustle unlike any other,
and down the line, even rock
could not stop to roll. In crashing
tide of chords that never learned
to move anyone's feet, we dance,
shake, and convulse.

Take a bullboat out in to shark-
infested water and learn
never stop moving.

THESE LIGHTS FLICKER AND FALL

At the start of the fall they hauled my little league
coach outta the bar. On the grimiest ship, he sailed
over to me, asked me how I was feeling, then drifted
back into a sleep that looked so inviting the bartender
got jealous and called the fuzz. As they drug him not
me out of the door, Coach rose up floppy as a salmon
in a suit made of banana peels, made eye contact
with me and said,

"CHUCK, WE'RE DOWN 1, KNOCK IT OUTTA THE PARK!"

Didn't have it in me to tell him my name is Vince.
Wanted him to flicker on again, to ride up in his brown
firebird jump out in his stonewashed jeans and too-
tight T-shirt. Tell us the next game is already in the bag
and so that's why he was already halfway in himself.

The bar at the end of the world is almost empty.
I'm in a booth, my troubles are handing out mints
in the ladies' room. Dan Snyder and Andrew Jackson
are lined up on the back wall falling in love with hate
all over again.

REDOUBTED

Don't act like you didn't see me coming;
I'm kinda hard to miss.

Probably thought they could get away with something hypersonic,
but see, baby, I'm quicksilver,
the caramel-skinned
sugar-sweet gingerbread man and
YOU'RE A MONSTER!

See this one

just happened to meet me in the middle of a victory lap.
Dead center in a celebration of the down, brown, and beautiful variety,
and this kid from a park nicknamed Cockroach
cannot/will not
let slick talk slip by.

This one sees
passive aggressive,
indirect,
unresponsive perspective and is way, way too familiar.

Know
that I have planted my sash in the ground
and have been waiting to count coup
on these abusive avian albinos for 150 years,
but they won't get the reference
cause maybe

this urban Rez rocket is just going
too,
too
fast.

Maybe this someone is channeling Drew Barrymore
and the rest of these country crack thin,
"I was being ironically racist way before Juliet Lewis was"
hipsters in headdresses.
Pretending she can't figure out why people are upset that she was photographed
wearing an apron from the king of beers while
also sporting plumage of my particular commercialized nightmare.

What lily in the flower shop can't understand basic cultural context,
let alone its potency?
But see, baby,
I bet they're catching on now.

Maybe we are tired of swimming
in a sea of dishonor and disrespect. Sailing to an ebb
and flow of appropriation that spans centuries,
we have been drowning in first world waters
since the first boats arrived. Becoming masters
at hunting whales of this kind, using the hollowed
out hulls of our decimated languages and cultures.

Help us to rebuild a ship made by our ancestors.
Work with us to destroy images that lock us into
a made-up history.

Know
that I am trying to dance away
Mr. Dynamite–style from a prairie full of feathery neon-colored
cartoons,

but it's rough.
The cape routine is tired,
all the purple and pink feathers from my
Generi-kee headdress have fallen off
I forgot the lyrics to "Pretendian: The Musical,"
this "leather" colored minstrel suit is too, too tight,
and the meek amount of sequins left
are holding on for dear life.

This one sees
that not acknowledging our own ethnocentrism
is like the occupy movement not acknowledging
they are occupying
what's already being illegally occupied.
See this one
doesn't buy it when the University of North Dakota said,
"Well, we had to keep using
the decapitated head of an Indian male as our logo,
it was the law."

Probably thought they would shock pushing
a breathing apparatus of fear
and red lightsaber of hate,
but
I will not be frozen in carbonite stereotype,
and these are not the Indians you are looking for.

SMALL CIRCLES

I wish I could take this conversation
home with me. I wish after I've cleared
my head that I could take you all out
of a pill bottle I keep all my best tokens
in. I would ply you with pens and paper
and let you live free on all the parchment
I'm saving for when the fat takers
have come for what's hanging from my waist
and thighs.

I wish I could take you to the parts
of my neighborhood that the hustlers occupy
and show them a you that pulls their interest but
swells that bit about them that they can't stand
to look at when the city is dry and they have
nothing left to slang but the bitter corners of a hazy
bag of shake.

I want to take your conversations with me to the job
interviews, and I would let you shine like you deserve
to. They in cramped awkward back office you would
help me to convince a worried management
that we deserve a shot that doesn't include barrels
and the ski mask way.

I wish I could take this circle to the Home
of my heart. I would convince my tribal council

to let us live in a HUD house on stolen seceded
lands. I would let them hear the ancestors
in your voices, and they would be convinced
you are the sleeping giant of our decimated future.

We'll never have hollow bones.
From depths of the colonized world,
with regalia sewn into the skin
of our upbringing that will never be shed.

Out to Adventure and Find the Me I've Hidden Away from Everyone

Cool air on my forearms lands
and asks what hair is there
to dance. Spin to see a wall
of flourish make the sign
for all clear. Exhale the smell
of fresh-cut grass. Reminds
me to float belly up down
the river of going nowhere fast.

Boss Wabooz thrives on a tucked

away butte and has found the way out,
is giving me notes on my own treasure
maps.

Melody of lime juicer invasion smooths
it all out just as Old Long Ears has set
rocking-horse racers loose into fields
full of lush creation. In the attic of glorious
foundation, smell every kind of paint
ever made and mixed. This is an eye-closed,
easy joy that never has to be repaid.

The tick ticking of the roller coaster
is an echo trapped in jar with 1,000
fireflies and two leaves that my baby
sister plays with in a state park
in Missouri. Have found my way back

from the lonesome valley and am filled
with the eyes and teeth of smiling
memories and ancestors.

ON A LAKE NAMED WARM PRECIOUS HANDS

Dual conversations in cat's
yarn ball made me flee scenes
of misery. Not paying attention
because the three of us are preoccupied
with distractions.

It's just me and the cautions
of the drive. Zig and zag in a fish
tank made of curbs and tar band
aids. I'm at the nonbeach on a lake
named Warm Precious Hands.

It happens, some quick shock,
and I'm here in a blink. Before
the why is remembered I'm ankle-
deep in cold lake. Whatever burst
made me flee my lodge along
the river is now floating away
as I make my way in past
the yelp of waist-deep water.

My hair, short, color of burnt
bones. Kindling a feast of cow,
corn, and potato, memories now
used as floatation device. Contrast
of hot hair and icy drink draws me
closer to wet horizon.

Full of mind, pull myself under
the birds, under the dogs and women
walking, under turn of bike crank.
Then free, zero boundaries now,
and to prove it do backflips in to loop-
de-loops into almost every last one
of Hammer's dance moves.

Only people who make eye contact
are babies. Collect their smiles
and coos as applause and standing
ovation.

THEY LEAP OUT INTO IRRADIATED BRILLIANCE

Symbol of the bat, lone etching in the gray
cloud of perpetuity is now lost within
brighter lights with better logos.
Many call out to hero and villain
with calls lit by imaginative longing.

Candles lit by LCD glow to timed dance.
Gleam of synchronized shimmer tells the story
of iron throne. As tale of might and myth
plays out before us, lightbulb to better strategy
sets the top of my head ablaze. Next time we
build the puzzle-piece island of Catan, it will
be I who calls out playfully

"I AM THE MOTHER OF DRAGONS!"

Calls are being answered, lit symbols in the sky dim
and let out the shadow behind rain and thunder-
filled pillows. The iron giants and their songs
of the new monster slow to a low hum. Open
the window and music of the city softens
as it stops to talk sweetly in my ear.

Helicopters at emergency speeds,
blinking with lights of crimson and indigo,
become leathery, volcano-mouthed hoarders
of lost treasure. Tonight I will let stories in through

my open bedroom window. Under cover of Moon's
star quilt, let these tales fill every part of me and shower
me with comfort.

The light of illuminated calls will warm us as they leap
out into irradiated brilliance.

1919

Article about wealthy women
in the world pops up while
I scroll down. The list includes
Caucasian women from every
part of the colonized universe.

Old money never runs out;
it just trickles down to your
descendants.

See a woman who was born
the same year my grandmother
was. My oldest relative, rage,
whispers new terrors that
I don't understand.
Then I do.
Close my eyes and try
to remember quiet mornings
with my Nay-Gah.
Squint to remember what her
voice sounds like.

Can't do it. Will never be able to.

Her, my aunt and uncles robe
up in motionless outline. Fade
as seconds build distance
between our eyes.

Then, questions with known
answers bubble like just done
soup.
Why isn't my grandma here
to see 2014? Why isn't this woman
in a house made of fortunate
outcomes without her legs? Why
are there articles about super-
rich white women?

Why am I reading them?

Pain and sorrow never run out;
they just flood the fertile lands
of your descendants.

VISITING HOURS

You have a call from . . .
first phone call from my soda
pop in five years. Mile marker
on the road of us zips by. We
inch closer to one moment while
miles farther from another.

Pep talk from ma with pops
in the background. Close
my eyes and wonder. When
I was on the other side
of the line did I sound as far
away as I sound today? Read
poems over the phone to my
cuz.
His response: "Crazy, don't
think you read that last one."
Me: "Hid in my heart, spills
out of my mouth."

Familiar tones from family
echo and fade as leaves rustle
in unison, sound like water
rapids. Hang up phone, lay
by the front windows
and pretend to be the best
rafter the world
has never known.

Earth-Hued Memory of Rest Lost in Song

When projects and the want
to earn just enough to survive
the next everyday apocalypse
morphs into long, stress-filled
days, my want to run
screaming into the soft caress
of queen size mattress knows
no treaty.

Sleep cycle, last bit of decolonized
me, does what it wants like Indigenous
second winter, reminds us we will
never make negotiations for its
people's surrender. Hollow howl
of airy and subzero expanse
sings my name and I two bustle
dance with ease and quicksilver
on top of these frozen letters
of title and familiarity, taken back
in time through memory bubbling
and volcanic.

In bright circle of foundation burn,
sleep and I made agreements
like head nods, fast and free.

Back then Sandman knew to back
away from laundry list of my

interests. In twilight, at reach
of darkest night and brightest
day, The Ishtabaytee giver
would never ask to dance me
outside upon video game release
as it knew my choice of story over
action would come in handy later.

There was one other dash
on napkin contact
of understanding. Indian women.
Even now, spirit of rubbed eyes
and footie pajamas dances
backward around the circle
when balance of my soul needs
to share my ears. There in shaded
round shape, dark rooms filled
with thumping base of my heart,
would turn off forever for painfully
skinny Indigenous woman who
just wanted to blend and share
a moment with me.

For them, and the thoughts of them,
the leader of the drowsy warriors
riding giant corduroy dogs
would hold his arm up and point
to the nearest and farthest butte.
Knowing that while in the moments
of shared connection, they should
never ever be run up on. These
are sacred fires that life
rides war-style on the side
of new gallop.

Offer the only thing left of my
uncolonized me. Quantum singularity
of stretching brown and black hair,
an infinity of wisdom yet learned.

Remember every last one
of your earth-hued faces
and smiles directed at me
without eye contact
that stop me and deer woman
cold. These hard to come by seconds,
given to me and only me like gift
of king size mattress on a twin
size box spring.

Complicated, beautiful, and filled
with spring, oak, steel,
and restful dream.

Because Every Day I Miss You, Madly

Just want you to come to my lodge,
laugh loud and tease me for being fat
and smart as a whip. Would open
the first door of me, so you could see
me, not as the disguised do but as my
sisters do, as my mother and father do.

Hoped for you to unpack your mule
and hold you up away from unending
drop of life. Sit here now, stare out
into memory and what could have been,
and think hard about all the unanswered.
The shadows that breathe and live on
short and curt answers.

When we had laughed hot through
a season of inclemency and cooled custard,
would feed you once more, make one last
joke, to hear your real laugh, finally.

Then I would go into the basement
of us, put on the robe of power and animal
and sing the words only my grandfather's
chopped-off fingers know.

Then in the real,
in the right now with the uncontrollable monster

just inches away, we would let the winter run
free without time as you do, confounding
the naysayers and everyone you allow
to pity you.

We would sit on the banks of our digression
and lost road as the river rose around us
to wash away your pain.

LEARNING TO CALL MYSELF HOME

Nothing is more beautiful, nowhere on earth calls to my heart more than this tiny part of the earth, mother to my people and our ancestors. My love for this place is buried deep into my genetic code. It grassdances up and down my double helix to the pulse of my beating heart. If you don't have somewhere like this, search the globe, find it, and let it fill you to the brim with strength. I miss someone strong today, someone who didn't take shit from no one. Everywhere, every inch of this Rez reminds me of him and his intelligence. My chubby brown heart is heavy and hot in the cold expanse he leaves in his wake. Today I'm the Sun slowly two-stepping into a giant lake of frozen water.

Mandaree singers taking me home today, all eight songs. I sometimes wish I stayed in Biz ya know. That's just cause my family is here and like a handful of really intelligent people. People that still can make me feel good through their FB status updates. I think about all of it, the good, the horribly bad, and as this car warms up I sing along with Mandaree, remember a Twin Buttes pow wow from my childhood where all my family was healthy and alive. Laughing and teasing, everyone's got a story about everyone else, and we laugh good belly laughs from the telling of our own hilarious history. The sharpest of wits, there isn't a breath in between jabs, someone is always ready with a retort, no one gets away clean. I learn fast that Mandans are quick-witted and throw words like Old West gunfighters, mouths smoking from the guns of our minds. Walking from the pow wow grounds to the lake with my sister to go swimming in the hot afternoon. Every year that walk to the water has gotten shorter and shorter. Last year the water had overtaken the grounds, and the pow wow had to be moved. A place called Like-a-Fishhook is slowly reaching out from our past, trying to save us all. I turn the music up in my car, get out, and dance hard for the last push up of a fast song, stop on time, point at my car, and laaaaaaaaaaaugh. I get in my pony and do something I haven't done since I moved away from where the earth meets the sky. I call myself because I need all my strength to continue. I need all my medicine because Man of Turtle has danced on. I know this because my brothers and I sang the traveling song for him. The suns coming up now, and I am being invited east.

Miss them all, and wish we could have grown old together, laughing and teasing at Twin Buttes as the water slowly rises up to save us all.

I'm up before the Sun again, been on cowboy time to long. Need to rest but I'm not done, so I put my biggest Kurt Russell mustache on and tell the empty kitchen that hell's coming with me! Lights go on, and I get told, "Shut up junior, and quit watching that stupid movie. Hahahaha-haha." I wake up, hearing that laugh like an echo in a cave. I wish burger time was open this early. WE RIDE! hahahahahaha

My ma decided to make the drive back to Biz. It's nice cause I feel like a little guy in the passenger seat. She has such great stories, but none are better than the ones she tells me about Uncles Leonard, Dale, Hooligan, Kelly, Delmar, Jim, and Josh. She has stories about my aunties, but they usually include her being naughty so she's reluctant to tell on herself. She is more than happy to share the misadventures of her brothers, and I am grateful, so very grateful to hear it all as the buttes zip by us in the distance.

Dancing backward hard today. Looking, searching for someone, anyone to meet my gaze. All the smaller monkeys heard the silverback's roar in the distance and are now intelligently being silent, keeping their dis-tance. Rightly so, as I wield this power, this medicine, this way carelessly and its warmth is deceiving.

It burns, burns, burns.

It's quiet, but I can't tell if this is solace, the sinus infection slowly eroding my ear cavity, or the calm before the storm.

IN AN OLD AND GOOD WAY

New steward on square
of independence begins
to build and blend into one
of the last and best neighborhoods
in all of the Southside of things.
Search and hunt for aged
carpenter tools, yesteryear's
technology. Time-tested
remodeling technique as bridge,
back to the starting point of when this structure

became more than a point of origin.

With same care and determination,
push hands one by one into backyard
of earth, mineral, and sustained
astonishment. From seed to stalk, bask
in the day's light, sun-kissed and worked
hard for growth of glorious bounty.
We will grow our meals as the Indigenous
Dakota had, centuries before these plots
would become swindled, stolen bits of this land's
recognized shared tragic history.

In an old good way, we've begun
simple fellowship with our neighbors.
Happily listen to story of previous
and sometimes missed overseers
of our current undertaking. Open

our doors to share progress as newest narration
from the allegory of this house.

Like observant ship's Captain,
we pay heed to fresh untested
waters. We are adding our names
to a diverse community that warmly welcomes
many into houses turned into homes.

On a Bridge No One Walks on for Help

In the city that holds my heart I stand
on a bridge connecting a path that is older
than this city that holds heavy pulse.

Worried someone passing by will think
I'm ill, I close my eyes and pretend to love
this place again and make cracked promise
that I will not back away from anymore
friends or family. Listen to the small bits
of words that spit out to change the fake
plastic nowhere into somewhere I used
to be from.

Made new ceremony in a kitchen that lies
about being my old kitchen. Asks me if I remember
a time when I didn't know it so intimately.
Cleaned my tongue with newly sprouted tobacco
leaves and wondered out loud to the glassware
how long it would take for someone to wonder
where I went if they were paying attention
to me instead of the outlines on the front sidewalk
I make.

The crickets in the park are the chorus of a high
school play, sing loudly so someone special will notice
them, and walk them home under dim yellow lights
while they hold sweaty hands. Drip a line back

into their neighborhood, still never want to break
the dam.

Climb the hill and a small fence, feel the whips crack
on the highway as they whoosh and whip sonic booms
past my face. Pull my hair out of its stunted old man
braid so that each follicle will not be scared of fast
invisible force and sing a song I think I heard
on the radio but was really an old message I saved
from my mom.

I have come to where unseasoned beauty sings with
tenured tragedy to give my sadness and storm of
tears to the passing wind because I do not know how
else to let it go. Write down and collect bad memories,
guilt, and left turns that should have been rights. Seal
monuments and mess-ups in plastic containers
with kidney stones, lumps of coal, and five years of unfinished
higher education. Think of wading out to dark waters
to let it all go, but the music of this night drowns.

Fake grasshoppers singing out for rayless embrace
and the echo these semi-trucks on this four-lane
super slab braid themselves down my back to form
my ghost braid. Whirring and buzzing calms
me as I bend over the concrete divider to see
the sparkle in the night, reach out to a fitful future
that shimmers and ripples from lean memory.

RISE AGAINST EBB AND FLOW

Wrapped up involvement in throw
back activism with a loud circle
of brown acknowledgment.

From tense deaf moments, we
share apology and uneasy embrace.
Here, we acknowledge mistakes
and concurrency. It is in precious few
seconds where our small fires become
prairies ablaze of shared future.

Within small circles on historic Franklin
Avenue, we claim one another and look
forward through different lenses.
We are together now like then, here
on The Ave. right now and in tight
pockets throughout beautiful
and sacred seceded lands everywhere.

We breathe as one waking giant,
and the exhale reminds me
to remember.

Once spring of our rebellion,
Franklin now shifts a rusty
trickle to proposed marketable
horizons. Packed in the stucco

of The Last Village, wedged
between old hustle and new
gentrification, we find, resolution.

We share, yet another forced cleansing.
Walk with blue corn balance, closed
eyed and take the first seconds
for myself in seven days. Count in Nu-Eta
hours of sleep I have slept. Gee-mah, six,
hours in Nupe, two, days. Rest will come,
but I am no longer asleep.

With swell of questions also came tide
of story. Not tale of myth or legend.
Round dancing to inbox were real
stories of others like us,
from others like us,
for us.

Messages of support, pride,
and undeserved thanks poured in.
Wide-eyed, read and could not stop
reading until I, too, filled every room with
The glow of *The Last Dragon*.

This amber ray flowed in from everywhere
The People rise.

This is good, this is best.

Let me create space now to thank a people
within a community not named after insect,
but for an insect's ability to survive
even nuclear winter.

To these Incredible Indians, I offer my unique
thanks. Much thanks to those who helped
to raise a scabby-kneed coyote into round
faced magician.

Let this glow fill all of you
for all time. Let us all remember
this decolonized voice,
wild and angry,
calling out to meet our past
and future on the road to the
beginning of an end.

Let this voice fill you and then,
sing, sing for all of us.

We hear you.

Still I Rise

I ride this rollercoaster of life eyes closed, head back, and hands reaching up to the twinkling ancestors in the sky.

With 90 seconds on the clock, I steal an inbound pass from the opposing team, shake the defender out his sad shabby socks, and make my way to 3-pt. land. I'm pursued hotly, and as I square up I see the shadow of all that is creep up to swat my dreams away. I close my eyes and see my relatives on a butte screaming my true name while shaking their coup sticks at me. When I open my eyes the darkness has surrounded me, and I put up a fade-away jumper that even makes Jordan and Alexie cry.

Then, I hear the crowd scream my name.